SOME SOUTHERN ADVENTURES OUTDOORS (AND IN THE KITCHEN!)

A Collection of Southern Adventures and Menus

STAN YOCKEY

Copyright © 2024 by Stan Yockey.

ISBN 979-8-9901403-1-8 (softcover)
ISBN 979-8-9901403-0-1 (hardcover)
ISBN 979-8-9901403-2-5 (ebook)

Printed in the United States of America.

This book is dedicated to my wife, Susan, and my southern hunting and fishing buddy, David. Both have left this earth – Susan likely singing in a Motown chorus and holding hands with the young children she loved so dearly, and David sipping his Sam's Club cola and puffing on a thin cigar. Susan always encouraged me to get away from the stress of the office especially if I was likely to bring something home for dinner! – and she secretly chuckled as I struggled to learn how to cook more than one dish at a time! David always wondered why I laughed so much, even though he had a pretty sharp sense of humor himself. I miss them both, so I hope that I have done justice to each of these wonderful people who helped me enjoy the outdoors in special ways.

Preface

The idea for this book sprang from some of the responses I got from several the publishers to whom I sent an earlier manuscript: Regional focus, they said, is very popular, so while they said that the concept and approach reflected in that first manuscript was unique and interesting, they felt that the same approach with a regional focus would be better received. My challenge, hearing those recommendations, would be to infuse some 'southern' culinary thinking into my admittedly 'northern' palette!

In "***Some Southern Adventures Outdoors (and in the Kitchen!)***," you'll find stories that relate actual outdoor adventures I've been fortunate enough to experience since moving to Savannah, Georgia in 1999. In pursuit of a number of birds, fish, shellfish, and small and big game quarry, I've truly been blessed to be in and enjoy first-hand the beauty and bounty of the southeastern United States.

You'll also note that, again, each story features a complete meal menu and the associated recipes at its conclusion. The message and intent continues to be to relate adventures about one or more particular wild species, then help you with ideas as to how to prepare them for the table in ways that are both appetizing and visually appealing. My objective remains to share a few interesting stories about the birds, fish and animals I pursue, and give you some menus and recipes that will help you enjoy the same game on your table.

To that end, there are complete meal menus of complimentary dishes rather than single dishes that leave you guessing as to how to make a complete meal. There are a number of excellent wild fish and game recipe and/or cook books available, but that very few 'connect the dots' between the dish made with the animal you harvested and other elements of a meal that complement each other, and I remain convinced that this approach will help you and your families and guests find the idea of eating wild game more appetizing.

In "**_Some Adventures Outdoors_**," I have tried to keep the recipes and menus fairly simple and straightforward, so you should be able to prepare meals that your friends and families will enjoy, even if you aren't an expert in the kitchen and your friends and family members aren't used to eating wild game. There are a couple of recipes that take a little extra time and care and are a little more complex than others due to the subtlety of flavors or texture of the game, but I am confident that you can prepare every one of these recipes with some planning and attention to details.

I hope that my enjoyment and appreciation of the outdoors and the bounty it has to offer comes through in this book, and that those of you who are outdoor adventurists should be able to either relive or imagine many of the memories I've shared – and then be able to prepare and enjoy a meal of your own harvests.

This book doesn't provide 'exceptions' or 'work-arounds' for the gamey or fishy taste some hunters or diners may have experienced. Perhaps everyone's taste buds are just different, but if you know or suspect that a particular animal won't be palatable, please think twice about killing it!

Separately, some readers will be glad to know that in a few instances the game upon which featured recipes are based can be replaced with 'domestic' or commercially-available equivalents without completely sacrificing the intended essence. For example, chicken (both meat and liver, as appropriate) can be used in place of rabbit (meat and liver), pheasant (meat), and partridge (meat); and lean cuts of pork can be used in lieu of wild boar. It's also perfectly OK to use store-bought fresh fish and shellfish when wild specimens aren't available. However, this is a book about wild game, so I truly hope that you can experience the recipes as they were intended!

In some instances you may decide that you'd like to use a particular recipe in a different menu. For example, the Smoked King

Mackerel Dip can be made with several other kinds of fish with firm white flesh. Just be sure to carefully adjust the marinating and/or cooking times based on the substituted ingredient(s).

Likewise, the salads and sides can certainly be mixed and matched as you see fit; the menu selections I've suggested work well together but are certainly not the only way to go! For example, the Chilled Sweet Potato and Asparagus Salad fits nicely into several other menus. Mix and match. Find combinations that work for you. Helping you enjoy every aspect of _your_ outdoor experiences is what this book is all about!

In closing, I hope you enjoy the stories and photos – independently from the recipes. They are all true, and I did my absolute best to share each of them with you in as interesting a way as possible. Where I had photographs of the adventure, they are included; where I didn't, I've either substituted representative 'stock' photos to help complete the overall experience or foregone pictures altogether. I hope that as you read each story, you'll feel as though you were there with me and able to imagine the sights, sounds, feelings and tastes that made each experience special.

Contents

Field and Kitchen Basics & Essentials

Every hunter or fisherman knows that proper handling and storage of wild game is essential to the taste and texture of the meat that eventually hits the plate. Sometimes time, weather, or other circumstances prevent us from doing everything exactly 'by the book' at the time of the harvest. Often, not being able to do everything that needs to be done immediately won't diminish the quality of your harvest, but certain basic steps should always be observed.

The Essentials:

Before we get into a discussion regarding the proper handling and storage of your harvests, it's important to address the importance of using the proper processing equipment, both in the field and at home. Based on my personal experience, there are five "must haves" to ensure efficient handling and quality results:

1. High quality and properly maintained knives and saws;
2. A clean, flat work surface in a clean environment;
3. Storage materials that fit the job and the game being processed;
4. High quality and properly maintained processing and cooking equipment; and
5. Fresh, high quality herbs, spices and produce.

Can you get by without one, some, or all of these items? Of course. After all, most of us have, at some point in our lives, not had the means to purchase high quality equipment or the knowledge of how much better and easier the handling and cooking of our game would be with the right gear. But, hopefully, one of the reasons you are reading this book is to learn something you didn't know that will help you do things better. And, if I do my job, you'll come away with new information and compelling reasons to use it! In that spirit, let's address these five 'must haves' in more depth.

Equipment:

High quality and properly maintained knives and saws are critical because they will enable you to field dress, skin, quarter or de-bone your game quickly and efficiently either in the field or at home. If you don't keep your knife (or knives) sharp, the job will be slower and harder than it needs to be. Quartering a two hundred fifty pound mule deer with the four inch sheath knife you just used to field dress it, for example, is way too hard – and none too sanitary! Or, splitting the backbone of an antelope you're your camp hatchet instead of a sharp, fine-toothed bone saw is both a pain in the rear end and will likely result in damaged or wasted meat. And, as a last example, trying to fillet a trout with your not-very-sharp pocket knife can be done, but it probably won't be pretty!

For all of these reasons, and after years of trial and error – some of which resulted in lost meat – I now use a matched set of knives and saws, and I keep them razor sharp and clean at all times. The manufacturer has worked hard to design and produce equipment of high quality with which an outdoorsman can handle even the most difficult field dressing, skinning or filleting, and processing your harvest efficiently. Of course, there are several equipment manufacturers whose products are of high quality and are well designed for the tasks at hand. For example, when I am hunting big game, I also carry (because my wife bought them for me as birthday and Christmas presents thirty-plus years ago, and because they're excellent knives!) a folding knife with a straight four inch blade, and exchangeable gutting and serrated blades, as well as a fixed-blade skinning knife if I intend to keep the hide: regardless of the brand, having tools designed for the job at hand will help you bring your harvest to the table with little or no wastage!

I also recommend – unless, of course, you are very experienced in processing your own game – that you obtain books and videos that explain proper field dressing and quartering and final processing of the game you intend to harvest. For example, after thirty plus years thinking that I was a pretty capable 'butcher' of the big game I harvested, I purchased and watched a couple of game processing videos and learned that some of the techniques I had been using weren't quite right, and that there were some new things I could do to dramatically increase my processing efficiency. Even old dogs like me are willing to learn new tricks when it makes our lives easier!

Processing Environment:

It should go without saying that a clean, well-lit work area with a large, flat surface is essential for processing your harvests – be they crustaceans, mollusks, fish, fowl, or large or small game, but many people (including myself for many years) make do with card tables or a hastily cleared-off garage work bench! Either will work, but the amount of extra time and effort that results from having to make accommodations for inadequate size and/or stability (not to mention cleanliness!) makes purchasing or constructing a right-sized work table worth whatever expense and/or time and effort is required!

So what should you purchase or construct? I have found that a three-foot by six foot hard-plastic table with folding legs and a flat work surface positioned under a three foot fluorescent light provides ample workspace, light and an overall environment that makes processing virtually anything I bring home easy. This assumes, of course, that a large animal, such as a mule deer, elk or other similar-sized critter will have been quartered before being brought to the processing bench! The table can also be easily moved, if necessary, for outdoor washing, storage, etc.

Separately, if the fish or game I'm processing takes up a majority of the table's surface, I'll have a card table on which I put my wrapping and storage materials – butcher paper, aluminum foil, freezer bags and the like – along with vinyl gloves, a bowl of warm water, and a clean towel.

A large cutting board is another key element of a well-equipped processing 'station.' However, it is extremely hard to find a cutting board that won't slip and slide on your hard plastic work surface, so I dampen towel that is larger than the cutting board and place the board on it before I begin. Another option is rubber matting – such as the material used to keep area rugs from sliding on hardwood or tile floors.

The cutting board itself should be 'knife-friendly:' made of hardwood (oak, maple, hickory, etc.) or synthetic material that will not dull the blades of your knives. For that reason, I do not use bamboo or teak. They are excellent in the kitchen for both appearances and trimming vegetables, but they are very hard on your game processing equipment!

Finally, unless your processing table is close to the freezer in which you intend to store the processed game, you should have a clean cooler with plenty of ice close at hand. The problems that come with time and temperature can come into play while you're processing a large harvest, so be prepared to either keep the processed meat cool until you can get it into the freezer or take periodic breaks to put what you've processed into the freezer before continuing.

Storage Materials:

Shellfish, fish, and meat will all last longer when they are properly processed and stored. One thing I learned – the hard way, through trial and lots of error, of course! – is that having the right materials at hand before you begin processing your harvests is critical.

High quality butcher or freezer paper and freezer-proof tape, along with a permanent-ink marking pen are must haves. Some butcher shops or grocery store deli or meat counters will sell you a roll from their stock, but in any event, an internet search will identify a number of on-line sources from which you can buy these supplies relatively cheaply, and each order should last you a season or more. Using freezer-proof paper will sever several purposes: first, it will prevent freezer burn, so storage life is extended and the quality of the meat will remain high. Second, it will allow you to wrap individual servings – one or two person portions or complete meals – and label them clearly so that it's easier to retrieve what you're looking for, rather than having to guess! After wrapping the portions, I then store several at a time in zip-lock freezer bags, and can remove them as needed, resealing the bag afterwards.

A good quality vacuum food sealer is another very useful tool that will pay for itself over time. Especially if you process several harvests (of any kind) per year, you'll be glad that you are able to protect them from freezer burn. Further, odd-sized and odd-shaped shellfish, fish and game harvests that are clumsy to wrap in butcher paper are a breeze with a vacuum sealer.

I also use seal-able plastic containers and half-gallon milk cartons filled with fresh, cold water when processing shellfish and fish. By freezing your catch in water, freezer burn is never an issue, and you can stack several containers neatly in your freezer.

Finally, I always make sure that I have an ample supply of heavy-duty plastic zip-lock freezer bags and heavy-duty aluminum foil before I begin a large processing job. As mentioned earlier, several portions individually-wrapped in butcher or freezer paper can be labeled and stored in a single one- or two-gallon freezer bag. Separately, I find that wrapping portions of smoked or cooked game in heavy-duty foil, then storing them in zip-lock freezer bags is a convenient and effective way to go.

Processing Equipment:

For the purpose of this section, "processing equipment" encompasses food processors, meat grinders, sausage stuffers, mixing bowls, and cookware. Your food preparation and cooking results just aren't going to be as good as they should be if you don't have and maintain clean, high quality processing equipment. Obviously, if you know that you have no interest in making sausage, you may not need to invest in a sausage stuffer. That said, a meat grinder can also be used to process other kinds of food: potatoes for gnocchi, squash for risotto, etc., and a sausage stuffer can, in fact, be used to make manicotti and other stuffed pasta dishes! My wife and I were fortunate enough to have a friend find a twenty-five year old Kitchen Aide mixer with meat grinder and sausage stuffer attachments, and we use it quite often to grind both wild and store-bought meats for pates, sausages, burgers and to stuff pasta shells.

It is also critical that the grinder and stuffer – including each of the components that are exposed to food materials – be thoroughly cleaned with strong soap and hot water, then dried, wrapped and stored in as sterile a condition as possible. Further, they should be washed and dried again before each use.

As for mixing bowls, I recommend (i) a set of sturdy non-reactive (i.e., micro-wave-proof plastic or glass) bowls of 1, 2, 4 and 6 quarts each, plus (ii) a plastic, flat-bottomed 3 to 4 gallon tub (into which ground meats can be seasoned and mixed prior to making sausage). 'Non-reactive' means that the material with which the bowls are made will not interact with salts, acids, enzymes or other chemicals that frequently come into play when soaking or marinating meats, or when mixing various ingredients during cooking.

Selecting cookware tends to be a matter of personal preference: weight, balance, exterior color (to match the kitchen and other appliances!), and other factors often come into play. To consistently put high quality food on the table for you, your family, and your guests to enjoy, however, you will be very happy if you purchase a few basic pieces:

- A 9 inch diameter, heavy-bottomed anodized sauté pan;
- A 12 inch diameter, heavy-bottomed, oven-proof anodized sauté pan;
- A 1 quart sauce pan;
- A 4 quart soup pot;
- A 6 quart or larger stock pot;
- A 9 inch by 12 inch [oven-proof] glass or aluminum casserole dish; and

- A 4 to 6 quart steel [lidded] roasting pan.
- Likewise, kitchen knives are tools that each chef must choose for themselves. Before you do so, however, consider the following basic ground rules when selecting your knives:
- First, each should be of high quality steel, so you can sharpen it quickly and easily and so that it will hold the edge.
- Second, I use and recommend four basic styles to will help you handle most any meal:
  a) A slicing and scoring knife with a five inch blade;
  b) At least one 'Santuko' knife with a five or six inch blade (I have three Santukos with three inch, four inch and seven inch blades, and I use them constantly – particularly to slice, chop and mince vegetables);
  c) A Chef's knife with at least a six inch blade (I prefer an eight inch blade to accommodate large roasts and the like);
  d) A cleaver with a six inch blade; and
  e) A high quality sharpener.
- Third, hold and get the feel of each knife to the extent possible before buying it. While most stores will allow you to return or exchange a knife that hasn't been used, once you've used it, it's yours, and trying to use a knife that is clumsy, too light or too heavy, or doesn't meet your expectations can result in handling errors and accidents!

Because you will want to protect your investment in these high-quality tools, and because you need to make sure that they are not used by anyone else who snuck into your kitchen and doesn't know how seriously they can cut the user, I recommend that you hang a twelve to fifteen inch magnetic bar on the wall in a recessed area of your kitchen and store these knives separately from your other 'every day' kitchen knives and tools. They are expensive to replace if damaged through misuse, and they can be very dangerous if used by someone who is not used to handling very sharp instruments, so treat them accordingly! As a quick emphasis of this point, my wife and I have agreed that she will not use my good knives: she has a tendency to not pay close attention to what she's doing and has cut herself several times with my razor-sharp instruments, and she has misused them on occasion, requiring extra time and effort to return them to the proper condition!

Alternatively, you can store your knives in a wood knife block – with the sharp edge of the blade turned upward (i.e., so that they are not resting on the sharp edge). This will help avoid blunting of the blade, but also presents the opportunity for an accident if you forget or someone else is unaware that the blade is facing upward! In any event, I recommend that the block be kept separate from any other knife blocks for both protection and safety reasons.

Fresh, high quality herbs and spices are essential. Generally speaking, a decent selection of herbs and spices can be bought in a well-stocked grocery store, but ordering on-line may yield a better result for those of you in the country or without access to a good selection. My wife and I currently have over sixty herbs and spices in our kitchen, and we'll use most of them at least once every month or two, but you can prepare all of the meals in this book with the following basics:

- **Salts:** Kosher and grey sea salt
- **Peppers:** Tellicherry (black) and white – medium ground
- **Garlics:** Fresh, granulated, and garlic salt
- **Basil:** Fresh and dried & ground*
- **Rosemary:** Fresh and dried & ground
- **Thyme:** Fresh and dried & ground
- **Ginger:** Fresh and dried & ground
- **Chilies:** Mild and Medium heat, dried & ground
- **Juniper Berries:** Whole, and dried & ground
- **Cinnamon:** Sticks and ground
- **Lemon Zest:** Dried & ground
- **Cloves:** Whole, and dried & ground
- **Allspice:** ground
- **Italian Seasoning:** dried & ground
- **Curries:** Mild & Medium heat

- **Paprika:** Spanish and smoked
- You should also keep these basic ingredients stocked:
- **Oils:** Extra Virgin Olive, Cannola, and Sunflower
- **Canned Tomatoes:** Diced, stewed, sauce and paste
- **Anchovies:** Paste and tinned
- **Rice:** Wild, brown and medium-grained white
- **Flour:** All-purpose white and whole wheat
- **Pasta:** Whole grain spaghetti, linguini, and spiral
- **Asiago or Parmesan Cheese:** Fresh
- **Soup Base or Stock:** Chicken, Beef and Veal

* Rebecca Gray makes an excellent suggestion that an easy way to have fresh herbs on hand is to buy potted plants available in many grocery stores and keep them on your counter or window sill, plucking a leaf or two as needed, then replacing them when all of the leaves have been plucked.

Regarding measuring cups/spoons, all I'll suggest is that the tools you select be easy to read, easy to use (i.e., NOT hanging from a ring or loop!), and that you have at least two full sets. I can't tell you how many times a menu has required measures of the same quantities of dry ingredients (flour, spices, etc.) and liquids (oil, water, cream, etc.), thus requiring me to pause to wash and dry the measuring tool before moving on! For a very nominal cost, you'll be very glad to have at least two sets at your finger tips!

Finally, I'll likewise leave the selection of cooking spoons, scrapers and the like to you – with one simple comment: make sure that the spoons, etc., you use are heat-proof. Many soft-plastic spoons and scrapers, for example, will melt if they are left in the pan – even when they're sitting in a sauce or other liquid base. A set of wood tools – especially bamboo – is versatile and heat-proof (unless, of course, you leave them on a hot burner or in the oven!), and several makes of silicon-based tools are available. Separately, because bacteria can live in furrows of wooden tools, be sure to clean them thoroughly with soap, hot water, and, occasionally, bleach after using them.

Handling Your Harvest

Crustaceans and Mollusks:

Time and temperature are the most critical considerations when bringing crustaceans (including lobster, shrimp and crab) and mollusks (clams, geoducks, and mussels) from the beach or ocean to the table. If you plan an outing with the intention of harvesting any of these delicate-fleshed creatures, prepare properly by bringing a bucket or cooler of cool, even ice-cold, water. Of course, the water and the ice can be kept separate, allowing you to add a few cubes of ice from time to time to help stretch your supply, but the sooner you get your catch rinsed and into cool water, the less likely it will be to experience spoilage. A lid or cover for the cooler or bucket is also a good idea so as to slow the time it takes for the water temperature to increase. If your plans are to be in the 'wild' for a long period of time, you should take occasional breaks to run your catch back to a large holding vessel once in a while.

Once your harvest is complete, it's just as important to get your harvest from its natural environment to where you can transition it from the cool water to the table, refrigerator or freezer in a timely manner. As soon as practicable, on a clean kitchen counter or sink, or at your clean worktable, re-rinse your catch in cold, fresh water, then process them for eating or storage.

My experience with clams is that they should only be frozen if vacuum sealed, and that they should not be refrigerated for more than twenty-four to thirty-six hours. Most clams are served immediately after being steamed until their shells open (and if their shells don't open after two or three minutes of steaming, they should not be eaten!), but the 'body' can also be removed from the shell, plunged into an ice-water bath, and stored in clean, fresh or lightly salted water in a tightly-sealed container for up to three days.

Fish:

As with crustaceans and mollusks, time and temperature are critical to maintaining the freshness and quality of fish. Fish should be 'gilled' (by cutting out the gills) or 'tailed' (by cutting off the tail) but not cleaned – and thus have their flesh exposed to airborne bacteria and heat – until or unless they can be stored in ice or ice-water, or wrapped and refrigerated immediately. Whenever I go out with a guide or on a charter boat, I ask how the catch will be stored until we return to port. On the outing described in "Cruisin' in Costa Rica," for example, I was pleasantly surprised to have our deck-hand tell us that he always 'gills' and bleeds, then cleans and filets the catch within a few minutes of bringing it on board, always has a reservoir of cold, fresh water on board with which to wash his hands, the filets, and the surfaces on which he filets the fish, and always has a large cooler of fresh, clean ice and clean plastic zip-lock bags so that he can store the filets immediately after he cleans them! This kind of care ensured that our catch was going to be of the highest quality when we returned to the resort.

Sometimes space and other factors prevent that degree of planning and care, and, your fish probably won't suffer as a result. In such instances, my strong recommendation is to leave the fish whole and un-gutted (so as to avoid exposing the flesh to the air), and store it in as cool a container or spot as possible. That is, if you have room for a cooler of ice, use it. If you don't have room for a cooler, store the fish in a shady spot and rinse it with cool water as often as possible.

Birds:

You've probably seen or read about our forefathers' method of handling game birds after the hunt: they hung the birds, usually by the neck, for several days. Modern science has taught us that you shouldn't do that! A host of bacteria, including e coli from a bird's intestinal tract, as well as mites from the bird's feathers, will have a chance to taint the meat while it is aging.

In fact, leaving a bird uncleaned for more than 24 hours in temperatures of fifty degrees or more risks spoilage. At the end of a day's hunt, you should dress, skin, rinse, and put your birds on ice. Then, if you believe that aging your birds improves their flavor, clean and rinse them thoroughly, then hang them in a cool, dry and clean place as you would a larger animal.

Personally, though, I am of the opinion that aging bird meat doesn't improve its texture or flavor. In fact, I much prefer making sure that the birds I harvest aren't allowed to dry out after cleaning. Marinating and/or seasoning them as needed to offset any toughness or gaminess will yield good, consistent results at the dinner table.

Many people discard the wings, thighs and legs of wild birds, but (unless they've been badly damaged by shot pellets) the thighs, at the very least, can provide an extra dimension in texture and flavor to many dishes. Alternatively, you can save them to use in soup, sausage and pates, so don't waste this excellent part of your birds!

Small Game:

Small game should be handled essentially the same as birds: they should be cooled – and kept cool – as soon as possible after being killed, and they should be cleaned and rinsed thoroughly within 24 hours (or less if the temperature exceeds 50 degrees). Once cleaned and rinsed, the animals can be stored on ice or in the refrigerator or freezer whole or quartered, at your discretion.

Also, if you like chicken livers – sautéed, deep-fried, or in a pate – rabbit liver is an excellent alternative. Properly cleaned and preserved, rabbit liver is mild and full of both Vitamin D and 'good' cholesterol, so don't forget to save it when you process your rabbit harvest!

Large Game:

Fortunately for hunters in most states, big game hunting seasons occur in the fall and early, when temperatures are generally lower than the rest of the year. This is, of course, to reduce hunting pressure during the animals' most stressful times of the year – winter – when forage is less nutritious and harder to find, spring – when animals give birth to their young – and summer, when the young grow and the older members of the herd eat plentifully in preparation for the coming breeding season and the hardships of winter.

One of the coincidental benefits of fall and early winter hunting seasons is that proper treatment and handling of harvested animals is easier, with less meat spoilage or loss to heat far less likely. The most southern states – Florida, Georgia, South Carolina, Alabama, Mississippi, Louisiana, Texas, New Mexico, Arizona, and southern California – are typically exceptions, with fall and early winter temperatures often remaining at fifty degrees and higher. Even in these states, however, proper planning and attention to the basics of field dressing and prompt processing will help keep your game from spoilage.

While an entire book could be written about proper handling and processing of your big game harvest from the field to the locker to the freezer, I would rather hit on a few basics and refer you to some excellent material already available – starting with "The Art of Wild Game Cooking" by Eileen Clarke and Sil Strung. In their book, Ms. Clarke and Ms. Strung provide an extremely detailed and thorough discussion covering the nuts and bolts of handling and processing big game animals. Separately, Outdoor Edge Corporation has produced the "Advanced Wild Game Processing" series of DVDs that take you from quartering and boning your animal to sausage making and beyond.

As for the basics – many of which are also addressed in "The Art of Wild Game Cooking" and "Advanced Wild Game Processing" – we'll focus here on the do's and don'ts of skinning, proper cooling of the carcass and meat, aging, and processing. Having a good grasp on these elements of big game processing and handling will assure you of excellent results in the kitchen.

Skinning

In "The Art of Wild Game Cooking," the authors make the observation that by skinning an animal in the field, the hunter has "…removed the animal's own sterile game bag and replaced it with a manmade one, one that is not nearly as sturdy and will not keep the carcass from drying out." Further, anything other than a good muslin game bag will not keep bugs out, so what does skinning in the field accomplish? (Speaking from personal experience, one important benefit is that you won't expose young children to the "horror" of having to watch the process – even by accident!)

So, unless you can butcher (process) the animal immediately or get the carcass to a cool storage locker to hang for aging, my advice is to field dress the animal and rinse the cavity as thoroughly as possible with clean water, but leave the animal in its skin. Once you are in a position to hang or butcher your harvest, you can then skin it and remove any remaining debris, cut out any bloodshot or tainted meat and move to the next step.

Proper Cooling

Moving to Georgia in 1999, I had to make several adjustments to my planning and approach to handling big game once I had it on the ground. When hunting feral pigs and deer in temperatures frequently in excess of seventy degrees, several accommodations helped make sure that the meat didn't suffer from spoilage due to heat:

- As soon after the kill as you can, field dress the animal and spread the chest cavity as wide as possible, then rinse it thoroughly to remove blood and any dirt or debris that may have made its way into the cavity during field dressing. Doing so will remove any undesirable body fluids – bile, intestinal material, etc. – and will start the cooling process;

- Have a source of fresh water reasonably close at hand. For example, when harvesting "A Mixed Bag," my hunting buddy and I were able to take our deer to the shores of Banks Lake within a couple of hours of field dressing to wash out the animals' body cavities. Later, when hunting the Savannah National Wildlife Refuge in "Three Little Piggies," we were always near fresh water creeks or the Savannah River in which we would be able to rinse out the body cavities of our game as soon as possible after the kill. When hunting far inland in areas where no water is readily available, I carry several one-gallon plastic milk jugs full of fresh water in the back of the car or truck and rinse out the body cavity as soon as possible. As mentioned earlier, a fresh water rinse will clean out dirt and body fluids that can increase the likelihood of spoilage and help cool the carcass; and
- Skin the animal as soon as possible, but not before you are ready and able to move to the next step – hanging or butchering. Especially if the temperature is below fifty degrees, you are not likely to suffer meat spoilage for twenty-four to thirty-six hours.

Aging

Aging meat has been a done for hundreds of years, even though the science behind it is not that old. Aging is, at its basest level, the process by which the collagen in meat is broken down by the enzymes that are also present in the meat, thus tenderizing it. If the animal you've harvested has little or no collagen, all the aging in the world will not make it more tender! Know, also, that the higher the average temperature during the aging process, the quicker the process will occur, so more attention – starting with regular inspection of the carcass to identify mold or odors – is essential. Butchering should be done immediately if any mold or even the faintest unpleasant odors are noted.

Generally, at average temperatures of forty-five to fifty degrees, a deer will have aged sufficiently in four to five days; colder temperatures allow and require a little more time, and warmer temperatures will speed up the process. Finally, if the air temperature is going to average below freezing, you will need to heat the area in which the carcass is hanging to keep it warmer – at least thirty-five to forty degrees is a good rule of thumb – or the aging process may stop completely.

I have never intentionally aged the big game I've harvested, and the meat has always been flavorful and tender. What I didn't realize until reading "The Art of Wild Game Cooking" was that, in fact, the animal was aging without me realizing it or thinking of it as aging between the time rigor mortis left the body and when it was processed. In almost all cases, excluding the very young and tender feral hogs we butchered the afternoon of the hunt, my animals have been aged – prior to skinning – anywhere from ten to twelve hours to two days until I could process them.

Processing

As suggested earlier, I strongly recommend that anyone who processes their own big game obtain books or videos on the subject. Videos, in particular, give you the opportunity to watch the process being performed by an expert, and will, I assure you, either teach you things you didn't know or correct things you may have been doing wrong – or both! From quartering and de-boning to the actual butchering process, using the proper techniques will ensure that you are able to save more meat and do more with that meat. As one quick example, "Advanced Game Processing" shows how to section out a hind leg differently than I had ever done it, yielding a couple of excellent roasts that I had never known how to 'extract.' The amount of meat was the same, but I was able to do more with what I had.

Once at the processing table with your game and your equipment in place, you're the boss. That is, you can butcher and package your fish, bird, or animal any way you want, based on what you intend to do with the meat. Here are a few suggestions as to what you can do for different needs:

Fish:

- Pan-fish: In the South, pan-fish such as crappie, bream, perch and the like are generally cooked whole, so processing them is easy. Gut, be-head and rinse the fish thoroughly in fresh water, then freeze them in milk cartons filled with fresh water. Plastic bags and foil are not recommended because the fish's sharp fins will puncture them, exposing the fish to freezer burn.
- Medium to large fish: Most medium-to-large freshwater fish – walleye, catfish, bass, pike, and trout (to name a few) – and many saltwater fish – rockfish, ling cod, Cabezon, greenling, sea bass, crevale, and the smaller species of tuna (again, to name a few) – lend themselves to being filleted: gutted, then cut along each side of the backbone down to the rib bones, then along the rib bones to the bottom of the body cavity. There is a row of bones that protrudes up from the backbone at about a forty-five degree angle into the fillet, leaving you the option of removing those bones with a pair of pliers or leaving them in place. If you leave them, be sure to warm your guests! Note: the only bones present from the tail-end of the body cavity to the tail are the vertical bones of the backbone, so a tail section fillet is always boneless.
- Large fish: There are additional options available when processing large freshwater and saltwater fish, depending on how you intend to prepare them.

For example, virtually any large fish, from lake trout, musky, salmon, medium-to-large tuna, swordfish, amberjack, etc., can be portioned into steaks by cutting at a ninety degree angle to the fish. If you plan to cut your lake trout, salmon or tuna into steaks, my recommendation is that you fillet the tail section (i.e., from the tail-end of the body cavity down to the tail), then cut the rest of the fish into steaks of no more than one inch in thickness.

If you plan to smoke your trout, salmon, Spanish or King mackerel, etc. you'll get the best results from filleting them, then cutting the fillets into manageable pieces before brining or marinating them. Here again, you can either remove the bones that remain in fillets before smoking or leave them to deal with at the table!

Birds:

With very few exceptions, I am of the opinion that game birds can be best handled and processed by field dressing and skinning, then removing the head & neck, the wings above the 'elbow' (i.e., the first joint), and the legs at the hip joint. Then, the legs should be cut at the 'knee' to make two pieces, and the remaining wing section should be severed from the body at the 'shoulder'. These pieces can then be stored separately for use in soups, sausages, coq au vin, and other dishes in which they will be cooked to the point of falling off the bone.

That said, if you know in advance that you want to roast a whole bird, remove the feet by cutting them off at the joint below the drumstick, and remove the wings by cutting them off at the elbow joint. You should then pluck all of the feathers, taking care to avoid allowing feathers into the body cavity. Unless you have (or have access to) a plucking machine as we did in "Mostly Mallards," plucking can be tedious and time-consuming. As one approach, some people pluck the large outer feathers, then finish off the remaining under feathers or down with a propane or butane torch by flash-searing them, then wiping against the grain with a towel to remove the residual ash and stubs. Chances are that you will not eat the skin after cooking, so this method works well and saves a lot of time. Either way, once you've finished plucking the bird, remove the head and neck before wrapping or packaging.

If you skin the bird and remove the wings and legs, you then need to deal with the breast by either removing each side carefully from the breast bone and ribs with a sharp filet knife or cutting laterally through the ribs to remove the backbone. In the latter case, the breast can either be cooked whole or boned out (filleted) prior to cooking.

Small Game:

The simplest and, generally, most effective way to process small game such as rabbits, squirrels, and other similarly-sized animals is as follows:
- Field dress and rinse before bringing them to your processing table;
- Skin;
- Remove the head just below the skull and the feet at the elbows and knees;
- Quarter as you would a big-game animal, removing the front legs at the shoulders and the hind legs at the hips;
- Remove the lower half of the rib cage by cutting laterally across the ribs just below the bottom of the backstraps; and
- Cut the body in half just below the rib cage. Even if the amount of meat on the lower half is small, it will provide plenty of flavor to the sauce, or can be used to make stock.

Large Game:

As we've discussed previously, I heartily recommend that you obtain a book or DVD that walks you through the processing of large game, but I can recommend a few basics in processing your animals:
- Field dress and thoroughly rinse the body cavity with clean, fresh water;
- If circumstances are such that bringing the animal out in pieces is necessary, skin it – either after hanging it in as cool a place as possible or by skinning it on one side then rolling it over, still on the skin, and skinning the other side – then 'quarter' the animal.

In true quartering, you'll need to: (i) split the chest open at the sternum; (ii) split the backbone down the center from the hips to the neck (or carefully cut the backstraps along the backbone and cut the ribs from the backbone using either a bone saw or a hatchet); then (iii) cut the body in half by cutting through the backbone just below the rib cage. Voila – four quarters!

For a large mule deer, elk, moose or caribou, however, quartering involves cutting the animal into more than four pieces due to size and weight considerations. When dealing with these larger species: (i) remove the front legs at the shoulders; (ii) remove the back legs at the hips; (iii) remove the tenderloins; (iv) remove the neck by cutting cross-wise just above the front of the rib cage; (v) split the chest open at the sternum; (vi) cut the body in half by cutting through the backbone just below the rib cage; then (vii) split the backbone down the center from where you cut the body in half to the neck (or carefully cut the backstraps along the backbone and cut the ribs from the backbone using either a bone saw or a hatchet and discard the backbone.

- If you can transport the animal whole, cool the body cavity as much as possible by opening up the rib cage and using ice if the air temperature is above fifty-five degrees;
- Skin the animal once it is in a clean and moderately controllable environment – relative to bugs, rodents and temperature;
- Age the skinned carcass by hanging it for a period of time consistent with the animal's age and body size, and with the air temperature between thirty-five to forty degrees and fifty degrees; and
- When the meat is sufficiently aged, proceed with butchering, removing and processing section of the animal at a time.

I realize that this overview doesn't come close to covering everything that a person new to hunting and/or cooking wild game needs to know, and that a veteran hunter and/or wild game cook probably already has their own views and approaches to certain techniques used to process and cook their harvests. In either case, my intention is to offer some ideas that may be helpful to anyone who loves the outd-oors and its bounties.

So, with these thoughts and suggestions in mind, let's venture outdoors to harvest some critters and see what we can do with them!

There Ain't No Turtles in Turtle Bay!

A couple of years after a new job brought my family and me to Savannah in early 1999, my friend Don wanted to visit so we could try some inshore fishing in the coastal tide flats. We would be fly fishing for red drum (also known as spot-tail bass and redfish), and weakfish (also known as speckled trout). I asked around for a good guide and was referred to "Captain Greg."

The day of our trip was clear and mild –seventy-five degrees, but with a steady breeze wafting out of the northwest in the wake of a tropical storm that had blown through earlier in the week. We quickly loaded our gear into Capt. Greg's boat while he checked his supply of flies and provisions.

As we pushed away from the dock and headed toward the Savannah River, Capt. Greg told us that we would fishing a large flat as the tide was changing, and that we would be navigating various channels in a shallow tide flat in the search for redfish and speckled trout along the reedy shores. The trick, he explained, was to locate the fish hunting the reeds for shrimp and crabs before the water began to recede and became too shallow for either the fish or us!

We raced across the Savannah River and around a couple of palm-covered islets to enter Turtle Bay. Capt. Greg found the channel that led into a small pool in which the redfish and trout could hide during the low tide. As we entered the pool, he cut the engine so that we could drift to the upper end of the still water.

Don was positioned on a flatform on the bow of the boat. Neither of us had fished for redfish or trout, so Capt. Greg quietly told Don to cast toward the far side of the pool, then strip the line in, causing the fly to look like an injured minnow.

I had tied on a buoyant streamer with long, bright white and blue deer hair hackle, which I cast further down-water so as not to encroach on Don's part of the pond.

It didn't take long for the surface of the water to explode under Don's fly, and he quickly found himself in a battle with a feisty redfish. Don fishes rivers and streams of Washington state for trout, steelhead and salmon, so a two pound redfish in still water didn't surprise him! Because we were both using three-pound test leaders, though, Don played the fish carefully, letting it take runs before guiding it back toward the boat. Several runs later, Capt. Greg deftly netted the bright bronze-colored fish, removed the hook, and released it back into the pool.

A few minutes later, a fish swirled behind my fly.

"Strip it faster! He's on it," said Capt. Greg, trying to keep his voice down so we wouldn't scare the fish.

I tugged the line a couple of times quickly, and the fly broke the surface of the flat water. Mere seconds later, the fish struck with a fury, grabbing the fly and heading for the deep water of the pool. I raised my rod tip just enough to set the hook without too much force. A couple of frantic runs later, Capt. Greg netted a nice eighteen-inch spotted trout.

"Not back for the first five minutes, eh boys," said Capt. Greg – who was actually younger than either Don or me!

"Fantastic," Don replied. "Is it going to be like this all day?"

"It can be," the captain answered. "We also might not see another fish!"

"Forget I asked!" said Don. "I don't want to jinx us!"

As it turned out, he hadn't, as we drifted down the length of the pool, hooking, playing, catching and releasing three more fish. By the time we can to the channel at the bottom of the pond, however, the water had begun to recede – quickly!

"We'd better get out of here," said Capt. Greg, "or we'll get stuck in the mud at the other end of the channel!" With that, he planed the outboard engine to keep a shallow draft and guided us back to Turtle Bay.

When he was comfortable that the water around us was deep enough to avoid getting stuck, he cut the engine so that we could drift across a shallow weed bed. Because of the strong tidal action along the South Carolina and Georgia coast, there is a lot of silt that keeps weeds from growing on the flats most of the time, but Capt. Greg knew this area had several mounds that hosted weeds – and a lot of baitfish and mollusks.

At Capt. Greg's suggestion, we changed flies to 'clouser minnows,' a pattern that mimics small shrimp and crabs, with large beaded eyes and the hook facing upwards to avoid snags in the weeds.

Don cast his fly over the top of the weed bed and began short, jerking strips. I had barely made my first cast when the water exploded around Don's line and a bright bronze redfish streaked away from us with the fly firmly sunk into its upper lip. Almost at the same time, a speckled trout hit my fly and began to race away from the boat.

Fortunately, both fish headed away from the weed bed, so we didn't have to worry about getting tangled in the leathery grass. We each played our fish gently to keep our lines from crossing and to keep the fish away from the weeds, and Capt. Greg was soon landing and releasing them.

As Capt. Greg began to stand up after returning my trout to the water, he hissed loudly, "Don, look to your right! Do you see the swirl? Flip your fly about ten feet over it and strip it back as quickly as you can!"

Don did as he had been told, but his fly fell a little short of its target, spooking a huge bull redfish Capt. Greg had noticed as it swam towards us. When the fly hit the water, the fish turned with a flash of bronze and headed toward deeper water.

"That fish was about forty pounds!" Capt. Greg exclaimed. "It's too bad you didn't have a decent shot at catching him!"

"I don't know if my leader could have handled something that big!" Don replied, "but I sure would have had fun finding out!"

By this time the receding tide had brought the water level to less than two feet, and Capt. Greg decided that we needed to head out of there or we'd have to spend the next ten or so hours waiting for the tide to fully recede and rise again!

Don and I agreed, contentedly, that our visit to a turtle-less Turtle Bay had been a day well spent!

Macadamia Nut-Encrusted Striped Bass*

Ingredients:

- 4 ounces (about 1 cup) coarsely chopped macadamia nuts
- ½ cup plain bread crumbs
- 2 tablespoons all-purpose flour
- ½ teaspoon medium-fine grind white pepper
- ½ teaspoon kosher salt
- ¼ cup butter, melted
- 2 Tbsp extra virgin olive oil
- 2 cloves minced garlic
- 2 striped bass filets, about 4 ounces each

Preparation:

1. Mix the nuts, crumbs, flour, pepper and salt together in a small bowl, then slowly pour in the melted butter, stirring constantly to ensure thorough mixing.
2. In a 9" heavy-bottomed, oven-safe sauté pan, heat the oil over medium heat until shimmering
3. Add the garlic and sauté until it starts to turn golden brown (about 3 or 4 minutes)
4. While the garlic cooks, (i) pre-heat the broiler, and (ii) rinse the filets and pat them dry with a paper towel.
5. Place the filets, skin side down, on a cutting board or a clean countertop, then spread the macadamia nut mixture onto each filet, pressing it gently into the flesh. Once each filet is coated, place them into the sauté pan, skin side down. Cook until the flesh begins to firm up – about 12-15 minutes.
6. Remove the pan from the burner and transfer to the oven/broiler. Broil for 5 to 6 minutes, or until the coating begins to brown.
7. Remove the pan from the oven/broiler to a cool burner on the stove top, then gently lift each filet onto a serving platter with one or two spatulas.

* Grouper and cod are acceptable alternatives.

Candied Acorn Squash

Ingredients:

- 4 acorn squash
- ⅓ cup butter, melted
- ⅓ cup brown sugar, packed
- ⅓ cup maple syrup
- ½ tsp ground cinnamon

Preparation:

1. Preheat oven to 375°F.
2. Cut each squash in half lengthwise, then scoop out and discard the seeds. Cut each half crosswise into 1 inch slices.
3. Arrange the slices slightly overlapping, in a lightly greased 13 × 9 × 2-inch baking dish.
4. Bake, covered, for 35 minutes.
5. Combine melted butter, brown sugar, syrup and cinnamon, and spoon mixture over the squash slices.

Hearts of Palm Salad

Ingredients:

- 3 tablespoons extra virgin olive oil
- 2 tablespoons tarragon vinegar
- ¼ tsp Dijon Mustard
- ¼ tsp kosher salt
- ¼ tsp coarsely ground black pepper
- 2 cups (one 14 ounce can) hearts of palm, drained and sliced
- ⅓ cup red bell pepper, diced
- ½ cup artichoke heart, drained and sliced
- ⅓ cup kalamata olives, pitted and halved length-wise
- 3 cups package mixed salad greens (baby spinach, endive, baby romaine, etc.)
- 2 hard boiled eggs, cut cross-wise into thin slices
- 1 cup cherry tomatoes, halved

Preparation:

1. Combine the dressing ingredients in an airtight container and shake vigorously to mix. Chill until the salad is ready to serve.
2. Combine the hearts of palm, peppers, artichoke hearts, and olives in a large serving bowl.
3. Pour the dressing over the palm, peppers artichoke hearts and olives, and toss gently. Cover and refrigerate for at least 1 hour.
4. When ready to serve, place the mixed greens on chilled individual salad plates, divide the heart of palm mixture evenly over the plates and arrange the tomatoes and hard-boiled egg slices over the top.

Suggested Accompaniment:

- **Chenin Blanc:** Dry Creek Vineyard – Sonoma Valley, California or Graham Beck Game Reserve – South Africa
- **Chardonnay:** 14 Hands – Columbia Valley, Washington

Macadamia Nut-Encrusted Striped Bass

64 "Day-Ed" Birds!

As I think about the positive influences being in the outdoors has had on me throughout my life, the memory of hunting upland game birds with purebred hunting dogs – our favorites were German Short-hair Pointers – a quail hunt with my son, Luke, is one of my favorites.

One early spring afternoon, my boss invited me and Luke on a quail hunt at Beaver Creek Plantation near Metter, Georgia, but on the morning of the hunt, he told me that he had to attend a meeting that would last most of the afternoon.

"You and Luke go ahead. Everything is arranged, and it's too late to reschedule," he said. I was disappointed that he wouldn't be there, but I knew that Luke and I would have a good time.

"Good Morning, Gentlemen. I'm LeRoy, and I'll be your guide this afternoon," said a fellow as he climbed out of a golf cart to greet us as we pulled up in front of the log cabin lodge. "Would you like to go shoot a few clay pigeons before lunch? We have a trap range just down the road" he said.

After a little practice shooting and a delicious lunch, we climbed into a truck lined on each side of the bed with three dog 'boxes.'

"We use two dogs for each set. Someone will bring us two fresh dogs between sets," LeRoy explained when I asked why only two of the six boxes had dogs in them.

After a drive of about two miles, the truck came to a stop in the whirling dust. We made sure we had plenty of shells in our shooting vests, as LeRoy hoisted two beautiful English Pointers to the ground: both "Rosy" and "Jake" were eager to go!

As we walked at a brisk pace to keep up with the dogs, LeRoy told us that they were from a blood line of pointers that had been at the Plantation for nearly thirty years, and that they had parented two litters of great pups together.

It didn't take long before Rosy snapped into a rigid point, her eyes peering intently into a briar thicket. Jake froze when he saw Rosy, 'honoring' her point. Did I mention that I love watching bird dogs work?

"Luke, you take any birds that fly to the right, and your dad will stay to the left. Birds up the middle are fair game!" LeRoy said quietly as we approached the thicket. A moment later, five birds burst from cover. Two headed left, one flew straight away, and the last two angled to the right.

I quickly dropped two birds with two shots. Luke fired at his birds, missing both.

Jake was off in a streak toward the two fallen birds, screeching to a halt in a cloud of dust as he nearly ran over the first one. He snatched up the small bird and brought it straight back to LeRoy. Rosy, however, hadn't found her bird, and was casting back and forth in the calf-deep grass.

"Day-Ed!" LeRoy shouted as he walked toward her. "Day-Ed." It took me a moment to realize that he was saying "Dead" as in "Dead Bird," which was the command we had trained our dogs to follow when seeking a downed bird. Rosy soon emerged with the bird in her mouth.

"What happened, Luke?" I asked as we regrouped.

"I don't want to make excuses, but shooting your gun is harder than I expected!' he replied.

"I couldn't hit anything with that big ole gun either!" LeRoy chimed in, chuckling.

We reloaded and continued on behind the dogs toward where the birds Luke had missed had flown. In moments, the dogs locked on point again. "Take your time," I said to Luke.

The birds flushed and Luke aimed carefully, hitting one of the birds. The one he missed landed again another sixty or seventy yards down-range.

"Try this gun," I said, handing him the 20-gauge as I took the 12-gauge. When the bird flushed again, Luke dropped it with a solid shot.

"I LIKE this gun!" he exclaimed as he lowered it from his shoulder. We quickly swapped his 12-gauge shells for my 20 gauge shells and continued across the field.

By the time we reached the third bunch of birds, I had dropped four birds in a row. Luke had only missed one out of his last six birds and was feeling a lot better.

As we crossed an open part of the field, Jake disappeared into thin air. "Where'd Jake go?" I asked.

'He's over yonder in a tub of water," he replied. Sure enough, there was Jake, rolling in half of a blue plastic barrel buried up to its rim and filled with water. "We have several tubs in each section, and the dogs know exactly where they are. They love to cool off when it's warm," LeRoy explained. Smart dogs!

By the time we had finished the first set, we had downed a total of 26 birds. As we sipped on a bottle of cold water, another guide drove up, loaded Jake and Rosy into boxes in his truck, took our birds, and moved two Brittany spaniels – Lulu and Beau, another bred pair – from his truck to ours.

After a short drive to another part of the Plantation, we climbed out of the truck and headed down a ditch. It didn't take long before LeRoy said, "Get ready boys. The dogs are gettin' birdy!"

Sure enough, Beau locked onto a bird, and, as Jake had done, Lulu honored Beau's point and waited, quivering, as we closed in. Three birds broke from cover in a whir of wings, and Luke adeptly dropped two. I drew a bead on the remaining bird and it crumpled in a cloud of feathers as the dogs sped off for the retrieve.

"Day-Ed!" LeRoy called, giving hand signals to direct Lulu to a bird. She knew not to give up as long as LeRoy continued his calls, and soon found the handsome male bobwhite.

Our shooting had definitely improved in the second set, and LeRoy was impressed.

"I didn't think you'd be able to shoot that well with that big ole gun!" he chuckled. "You boys killed almost every bird in this set.

Indeed, when we got back to the truck and emptied our vests, LeRoy counted 38 birds. Added to the 26 in the first set, we had, unbelievably, 64 Day-Ed Birds!

French Onion & Shi'itake Mushroom Soup

Ingredients:

- 2 Tbsp butter
- 4 medium sweet or red onions, halved laterally then thinly sliced vertically
- Kosher salt and coarsely ground black pepper, to taste
- **½ cup Marsala wine**
- 6 cups beef soup base or stock
- 2 cups water
- **¼ pound (about 2 cups) sliced shiitake mushrooms with stems removed and discarded**
- 1 loaf of French bread (or a baguette), sliced into ¼" discs
- 2 tsp minced garlic
- 1 Tbsp extra virgin olive oil
- 1 cup shredded smoked cheddar cheese

Preparation:

1. Melt the butter over medium heat in a 4 quart soup pot. Add the onion and a little salt and pepper. Reduce the heat to medium low and cook, stirring occasionally to prevent charring, for 35 to 40 minutes – until the onions turn light brown. As long as they don't char, the longer the onions cook, the sweeter they will become.
2. Add the wine, stock, water and mushrooms to the pot and stir, scraping the bottom of the pan to loosen any pieces stuck to the bottom of the pan. Bring the mixture to a boil, then lower to a simmer and cook for 35 minutes.
3. Preheat the broiler.
4. Place the bread discs on a foil-lined broiler pan and toast them under the broiler.
5. While the bread is toasting, mix the garlic and olive oil together, and spread a spoonful on each toast disc when it comes out of the oven.
6. Place four oven-proof soup bowls on a cookie sheet and ladle soup into each bowl, place two toast discs on top of the soup, and sprinkle on a small handful of the grated cheese. Slide the cookie sheet under the broiler and cook until the cheese melts – about 2 to 3 minutes – then serve immediately.

Broccoli Florets w/Garlic and Pimentos

Ingredients:

- 1 cup water
- 3 cups rinsed broccoli florets
- 3 garlic cloves, peeled and minced
- ¼ cup pimento slices
- 2 Tbsp butter
- Kosher salt and coarsely ground black pepper, to taste

Preparation:

1. Bring the water to a boil in a medium sauce pan with a steamer insert or basket.
2. Place the broccoli, garlic and pimento slices in the steamer insert or basket, cover, and steam until the broccoli florets are tender – about 12 minutes.
3. Remove the pan from the burner and transfer the broccoli, garlic and pimentos to a serving bowl. Add the butter and the salt & pepper and serve with the quail.

Mixed Spring Greens & Red Onion Salad w/ Raspberry Balsamic Vinaigrette

Ingredients:

- ½ cup extra virgin olive oil
- ½ cup raspberry balsamic vinegar
- 1 clove garlic, minced
- 1 tsp ground mustard
- ½ tsp dried thyme
- 1 Tbsp sugar
- Kosher salt and coarsely ground black pepper, to taste
- 3 cups mixed greens leaves, washed and drained
- ½ red onion, thinly sliced cross-wise

Preparation:

1. In a small mixing bowl, whisk together olive oil, white balsamic vinegar, garlic, mustard and sugar. Season to taste with salt and black pepper. Chill in the refrigerator before serving.
2. Arrange the lettuce leaves on individual serving plates and top with a few onion slices.
3. Drizzle about 1 tsp of the dressing over each plate, reserving the rest for the table.

Bob-White Quail Braised in Cognac w/ Peach Reduction

Ingredients:

- 4 Quail, thoroughly plucked and cleaned
- 3 Tbsp olive oil, divided
- 6 Tbsp butter, divided
- ¼ cup dry vermouth
- ½ cup thinly sliced peaches
- 4 Tbsp cognac or brandy, divided
- Kosher salt & coarsely ground black pepper, to taste

Preparation:

1. In a large, heavy-bottomed pan, heat 2 Tbsp of the olive oil and 3 Tbsp of the butter over medium heat until hot.
2. Brown the quail on both sides, then reduce the heat to medium-low. Add the vermouth, cover and braise for 25-30 minutes.
3. In a separate sauté pan, melt 2 Tbsp butter and 1 Tbsp of the olive oil. Add the peach slices and 2 Tbsp of the cognac or brandy, and sauté over medium-low heat, stirring occasionally.
4. Returning to the quail, increase the heat to medium-high and add the preserves, the remaining butter, and salt and pepper to taste. Add the peach mixture, then stir until the sauce is well blended, basting each quail gently. Reduce the heat to medium-low, cover, and simmer until the quail are fork-tender.
5. Remove the quail to a serving platter and cover loosely with foil. Skim off any fat and add the remaining cognac or brandy. Stir until the mixture bubbles, then remove to a gravy boat and serve with the quail.

Suggested Accompaniment:

- **Rose:** Apothic (Healdsburg, California)
- **Chardonnay:** Yalumba (South Australia)

French Onion Soup Cooking in Progress!
Quail w/Peach Reduction Broccoli Florets w/Pimentos

Power-Line Poultry

The turkey season was winding down quickly, and in mid-May, conventional wisdom said that the hens had been bred and the gobblers had shifted their attention to eating grasshoppers and frogs. Regardless, my hunting and fishing buddy, David, subscribed to the old adage that any day outdoors was better than one indoors!

It was this thought in mind that David and I agreed to meet early the next morning to spend another hot, humid day at our nearby hunting club lease looking for love-lorn or feeding tom turkeys.

Coffee cups in hand, we arrived at the property about a half hour before dawn, then proceeded to the trail head that led to the dry swamp bottom in which we'd seen turkeys off and on during the season. We donned our gear, grabbed our guns and decoys, and headed down the trail as first light painted the eastern sky. It was a beautiful scene we'd enjoyed several times over the past two years since meeting and becoming hunting and fishing friends.

Although temperatures in the area had risen to daytime highs of 85° F and nighttime lows of 60° F, it was noticeably cooler in the swamp bottom we would hunt that morning. We headed to different areas of the glade, using our flashlights to guide the way to our respective ground blinds.

Upon reaching my blind, I placed my gun and backpack next to a folding chair, then unzipped the front and side windows before stepping back out to go place three hen turkey decoys about twenty yards in front of the blind. I could see David's flashlight beam bobbing in the darkness on the other side of the glade as he, too, set out his decoys.

Within minutes of returning to my blind to settle in for the hunt, the morning light began to give shape to the trees in the swamp bottom as dawn began to arrive. I heard a loud owl hoot from David's direction as he tried to elicit a 'shock gobble' from any tom turkeys that might be nearby. Only silence followed, though, so I began to yelp on my cedar box call. A few minutes later, David also began to yelp, hoping to draw any toms in the area to his decoys.

And so it went for the next two hours or so – yelps, then listen; yelps then listen. At one point, David changed his tactics and gave out a loud gobble, hoping to bring any jealous birds to his blind. Still nothing.

After almost three hours, we had both decided that if there were any toms in the area, they weren't interested in what our decoys were saying, and we emerged from our blinds, stretched, and retrieved our decoys.

A few minutes later, we met up on the trail leading out of the swamp

"What now?" I asked, deferring to David's vast experience as a turkey hunter.

"Let's have a little breakfast, then head over to the power line," he replied. The power line cut through the back third of the property, and the club members had planted several food plots within rifle range of each of the three blinds placed along the edge.

By this time, the temperature had risen to nearly eighty degrees, so when we reached the car we were more than ready to peel off our jackets. David started the car and cranked up the air conditioning as we ate granola bars and sipped on cold Gatorade[R].

"When we get near the powerline," I said as we got underway, "I'd like to get out of the car before we round the last bend and sneak up on the first food plot." On a couple of prior occasions, we had driven around that last bend and scared feeding turkeys. I figured that by sneaking up on foot, with a large bramble patch blocking their view, any turkeys out feeding could be caught by surprise.

David stopped the car as we neared the bend, and I quietly slipped out, loaded my gun, and started creeping slowly toward the food plot.

I was almost flabbergasted when I saw several of the large birds feeding in the short grass! If I could see them, however, they would be able to see me, so I froze until the birds facing the road turned. I lowered myself to almost a crawl, and altered my path so that I was hidden by the brambles. My heart was pounding, and I hoped that I would be able to see if there was a tom in the bunch before David rolled around the corner!

Sure enough, there was a very nice tom a few yards away from the rest of the flock. He was facing toward them as he fed, letting me sneak a little closer. By this time, most of the hens had begun filtering into the woods at the edge of the plot, and I knew that the tom would soon follow.

I brought my side-by-side 12-gauge shotgun to my shoulder and carefully slid to my right to clear the brambles. Fortunately, the tom still hadn't seen me, and I was feeling pretty sure that I could get a shot off without spooking him. He was, though, nearly fifty yards away, so it would be a long shot!

Blowing out my breath to calm myself for the shot, I slipped off the safety, took careful aim, and pulled the trigger.

"Boom!" My gun roared and the bird stumbled as he started to run toward the trees. I rose to run after him, but by the time I cleared the brambles, he had disappeared into the trees. I jumped the small ditch between the road and the food plot and ran toward where he would have entered the trees.

Suddenly, several birds launched into the air, flying nearly straight up to clear the trees as they fled. It caught me by surprise, so by the time I was able to stop, release the safety and take aim at the last bird – a tom – they were easily fifty to sixty yards away and moving fast!

I pulled the trigger, but it was clear that the shot was too far, and that the birds had escaped. Disappointed, I turned back toward the road to see David pulling slowly around the corner.

"Did you get one?" he asked from behind his rolled-down window.

"I think so, but I can't be sure until I look more closely. I grabbed two more shells from my vest, reloaded, and headed back toward the woods.

Starting my search where I was pretty sure the bird had entered the trees, I scanned the ground to my left, right and straight ahead. Nothing. But the trees were very thick, so I knew that I would have to take my time and be thorough if I was going to find the tom – assuming that he was, in fact, mortally wounded.

After about fifteen minutes of careful searching, I backed out of the woods where I had entered and moved several yards to my left – closer to where the bird was when I made the first shot. I had only taken a step into the trees when I saw him, clearly dead, lying at the base of a small pine tree!

When I emerged from the forest carrying the big bird, David let out a whoop.

"You got him! Congratulations!" he called out.

"Yep, but he had me pretty worried," I replied. "I just miss-guessed the spot where he ran into the woods!"

"I heard you shoot twice," David said.

"Yeah, probably a bad decision," I replied. "The rest of the flock flushed as I ran toward them and I tried to shoot a second tom, but they were too far out by the time I could shoot."

"Well, you got the bird you were after to begin with, so that's pretty good!" he replied.

By this time, the temperature had risen further to nearly ninety degrees, so after taking a picture of the handsome bird, we decided to call it a day. To this day, I have great memories of my 'power line poultry.'

Turkey Liver Pate

Ingredients:

- ½ lb livers (as fresh as possible)
- 1 egg, hard boiled
- 1 large shallot or ½ onion, chopped
- 6 tablespoons duck fat
- 1 tsp smoked sea salt
- fresh ground pepper to taste

Preparation:

1. In a small pan, melt half the margarine over medium-low heat. Add shallots, and cook over low heat until caramelized, about 10-15 minutes. Set aside.
2. Melt the rest of the margarine in the pan and add the livers. Saute over medium heat until livers are no longer pink in the center, about 5 minutes or so.
3. Put the livers and the egg in a food processor, and pulse just until coarsely chopped (do not over process). Add the shallots, and pulse a few more times to distribute. Add salt and pepper to taste. Serve with crackers or toast points

Braised Fennel, Carrots and Apples

Ingredients:

- 1 Tbsp olive oil
- 2 cups fennel bulb, washed and cut cross-wise into ¼ inch slices
- 2 cups carrots, washed, peeled and cut into thin 2 inch strips
- 1 cup red onion, washed, peeled and coarsely chopped
- 2 cups Granny Smith apples, washed, cored and thinly sliced
- ½ cup apple cider
- ¼ cup apple cider vinegar
- ¼ cup honey
- 2 Tbsp brown mustard
- 2 Tbsp fresh basil, coarsely chopped
- Kosher salt and coarsely ground black pepper, to taste

Preparation:

1. Heat the olive oil in a medium sauté pan over medium heat and cook the fennel, carrots and onion, stirring often, until they begin to caramelize.
2. Add the apple slices, juice, vinegar, honey and mustard and stir gently to integrate. Cover and cook for 10 minutes, then uncover and cook until the liquid is absorbed and the vegetables are glazed.
3. Transfer to a serving bowl, sprinkle on the basil, salt and pepper and toss gently, then serve.

Turkey Breast with Fettuccini and Mushrooms

Ingredients:

- 1 tsp vegetable or olive oil
- 2 Tbsp butter, divided
- 1 deboned turkey breast, sliced across the grain into ½" thick medallions, then pounded to ¼" thickness
- 1½ tsp kosher salt, divided
- 1 tsp freshly ground black pepper, divided
- 2 scallions, diced coarsely with white and green parts separated
- 1 lb cremini mushrooms, stems removed and sliced thinly
- 1 cup chicken broth, divided
- ⅓ cup Marsala wine
- 2 quarts cold water
- ½ pound (dry) whole wheat fettuccine pasta
- ¼ cup half and half
- 2 Tbsp fresh parsley, chopped finely

Preparation:

1. Season the turkey medallions on both sides with 1 tsp of the salt and half of the pepper.
2. Heat the oil and half the butter in a large sauté pan over medium heat until the oil shimmers and the foam begins to subside.
3. Saute the turkey medallions for about 4 minutes on each side. Remove them to a plate and cover with foil.
4. Add the other half of the butter to the pan, then add the white parts of the scallions and the mushrooms. Saute for 3 or 4 minutes, then add the remaining salt and pepper. Continue cooking until the moisture from the mushrooms cooks off, then add half of the broth and the Marsala. Simmer until almost completely evaporated.
5. Bring the water, oil and salt to boil in a 4 quart stock pot; add the fettuccine and boil for 10 minutes.
6. Drain the pasta in a colander, then transfer it the saute pan. Add the remaining broth, the half and half and the turkey medallions. Simmer until the medallions are reheated, then transfer the entire mixture to a serving bowl. Sprinkle the chopped parsley over the mixture and serve immediately.

Sauteed Green Beans w/Orange-Sesame Dressing

Ingredients:

- ¼ cup sesame oil
- 3 Tbsp freshly squeezed orange juice
- 1 Tbsp low sodium soy sauce
- 1 tsp freshly grated ginger
- 1 Tbsp agave nectar or honey
- 2 tsp orange zest
- 2 tsp toasted sesame seeds

Preparation:

1. Whisk together all of the ingredients except the beans in a medium mixing bowl.
2. Cover and refrigerate for at least 30 minutes.
3. Steam the beans until fork-tender, then transfer to a serving bowl.
4. Remove the dressing from the refrigerator and stir before serving with the beans.

Suggested Accompaniment:

- **Beer:** Ice-Cold Dos Equis with a lime wedge
- **Pinot Grigio:** Monte Maria – Chile

Turkey Breast with Fettuccini and Mushrooms

Crime Scene Swine!

Having been introduced to feral pig hunting the prior year, I was excited when a member of my work team handed me a flyer from the horse ranch she and her husband frequently visited. The flyer wasn't about horse riding; as it happened: the ranch was also a hunting camp when deer and hog hunting was legal. And, to generate some off-season revenue, the ranch was offering half- and full-day feral pig hunts at a discounted rate. Perfect, I though to myself, wondering if I could get my son, Luke, or a friend to come along with me. Luke was in college and working full time, so he wasn't able to get free, and the couple of friends I asked couldn't come up with the money for two half-day (one afternoon and one morning) hunts. "More for me," I thought to myself as I called the ranch owner, a genial fellow named Hayward, to book my hunt.

The following week, I packed my hunting gear into the car and headed out on an easy hour and a half drive to Estill, South Carolina. Hayward had advised me that I would need a South Carolina hunting license, so I stopped in Estill to buy the license before heading to the ranch.

Another half hour later, I pulled into the long entry drive of Cedar Knoll Plantation. Hayward met me as I pulled up to the rustic lodge and we quickly stowed my gear in a cozy room. We chatted for a while as he explained the operation to me: each hunter could take one animal per 'sit' or be charged $300.00 for each additional animal. That sounded fair to me, even though I would have loved to shoot more than one pig if I got the chance!

Around two thirty, after I had range-checked my .243 caliber rifle's accuracy, Hayward and his camp manager, Billy, led me to

Hayward's truck; Billy then climbed into a diesel 'dump' truck whose bin was half full of corn.

"It's your first time with me, and there's only one other person hunting today, so I'm going to treat you to "the Jungle," Hayward said as we headed out. He leases three separate areas of land, two of which are fairly near the ranch and the third being the Jungle. "We named it the Jungle because it's down near the Savannah River and it's pretty dark and dense," he explained. "We have eight stands, but with the wind the way it is this afternoon, only a couple will work."

"You're the boss!" I replied, not knowing where we were going, and figuring that he knew what he was talking about. The drive to the Jungle took about thirty minutes, plus another fifteen to get to the stand Hayward had selected for me. As I climbed out of the truck, I could hear Billy rumbling towards us. Looking back, I saw the bin on the truck bed tilt backward and drop a line of corn in the road as he drove toward us. He stopped about forty yards from the tripod stand from which I would wait for a pig to appear, drove past us, and continued dropping more corn when he was forty yards out. Once he finished the drop, he turned the diesel around and followed Hayward back toward the gate.

It was nearly three thirty when I finally climbed up the ladder of the tripod. I'm not afraid of heights, but I have to say that sitting on a small seat perched fifteen feet in the air wasn't exactly easy for me at first! Fortunately, there was a rail that circled three quarters of the seat, and a seat belt, so I settled in hoping for some visitors to drop by!

It didn't take long before I heard, and then saw, a herd of black and spotted pigs – mostly youngsters to adolescents – come rambling up the road toward the corn in the road. There were, though, four very nice young boars that I guessed would weigh around a hundred and fifty pounds each.

Knowing that I could only shoot one on this sit, though, I decided to just watch them being pigs for a while. They were, in fact, pretty comical! The sows with piglets would chase the little ones around, and the piggies would squeal in delight at the game.

The sows and the young boars were more interested, though, in snuffling up as much corn as they could while the little ones played.

They moved toward me, essentially vacuuming up the corn as they went, and it was a hilarious scene, until a fox trotted out of the brush about fifty yards from the pigs. Boy did that cause a ruckus! The bigger sows charged up the road toward the fox while the smaller sows herded the little ones into the underbrush. The fox whirled and disappeared back into the undergrowth, but the damage was done – there wasn't a pig to be seen!

I sat, staring at the empty road, for nearly thirty minutes, kicking myself for not shooting one of the boars when I had the chance. Just when I had given up for the afternoon, though, the herd came snuffling and grunting out of the woods to resume their feast!

I wasn't going to dilly-dally this time, and lowered my rifle to shooting position, settling on the ear of one of the handsome young boars. A gentle squeeze of the trigger, a loud boom, and the pig lay dead in its tracks! The other pigs scattered, not knowing what had happened, but I was not prepared for what came next!

After only about five minutes of panic, the rest of the herd returned and continued eating as if nothing had happened and their comrade was merely taking a snooze! The other boars, the sows, and even the piglets scooped up corn until the roadbed was bare. Then, with the corn gone, they galloped into the jungle on the other side of the road and were gone.

When Hayward came to collect me right at dark, I told him about the crazy scene, and we both had a good chuckle. With my gear stowed, we drove down to where the boar lay and admired the healthy animal. As I grabbed the hind two legs and Hayward took the front legs to lift the pig into the bed of the truck, we both burst out laughing: The pig had fallen on top of a bunch of corn, then the other pigs had eaten everything up to and around his body, leaving what looked like a crime scene sillouette – in reverse!

Broiled Romaine Hearts with Anchovy Dressing

Ingredients:

- 10 to 12 ounces fresh spinach, washed and torn into bit-size pieces
- ¼ cup minced red onion
- 6 radishes, washed and thinly sliced
- 2 hard-boiled eggs, peeled and rinsed: 1 chopped and 1 sliced cross-wise
- 4 slices smoked bacon
- 1½ Tbsp bacon fat
- 1½ Tbsp sugar
- 3 Tbsp apple cider vinegar
- 1 Tbsp water
- ½ tsp kosher salt
- ⅛ tsp coarsely ground black pepper

Preparation:

1. Place torn spinach in a large bowl.
2. Add onions and radishes and refrigerate, tightly covered, for 2 to 3 hours.
3. Fry the bacon in a medium saute pan until crisp; transfer bacon to a plate covered with a paper towel and reserve the fat.
4. Combine the fat with the sugar, vinegar, water, salt and pepper in a micro-wave safe container and mix thoroughly, then refrigerate until just before serving.
5. When ready to serve, microwave the dressing on high for 30 to 45 seconds, or until mixture boils. Mix the chopped egg into the spinach leaves, then pour the hot dressing over greens mixture and toss lightly.
6. Top with the sliced egg and crumbled bacon and serve.

Oven-Roasted Asparagus

Ingredients:

- 3 Tbsp extra virgin olive oil
- 1 pound fresh asparagus, rinsed and dried, then trimmed to remove woodsy bases
- 1 Tbsp granulated garlic

Preparation:

1. Place the olive oil in a flat, shallow dish or pan.
2. Roll the asparagus stalks in the oil to coat each stalk thoroughly, then sprinkle the garlic evenly over the stalks. Roll the stalks as needed to ensure even coverage.
3. Transfer the stalks to a lightly greased cookie sheet and place it on the lower rack of the oven when the roast boar leg is done. Roast asparagus for 15 minutes, then transfer to a serving dish and serve with the roast boar leg and olive mashed potatoes.

Braised Wild Boar Shanks

Ingredients:

- 4 wild boar shanks,
- 1 pinch kosher salt
- 1 pinch black pepper
- 2 teaspoons powdered cocoa
- 2 tablespoons plus ½ cup flour, divided
- 2 ounces extra-virgin olive oil
- 2 carrots, sliced crosswise
- 3 celery stalks, sliced crosswise
- 1 medium yellow onion, coarsely chopped
- 3 garlic cloves, minced
- 1 12 ounce bottle hard apple cider
- 2 Tbsp Worcestershire sauce
- ½ cup beef stock
- 2 Tbsp tomato paste
- 1 teaspoon Kitchen Bouquet browning and seasoning sauce
- 2 bay leaves
- 1 tsp fresh thyme
- 2 Tbsp butter, softene
- Zest of 2 lemons

Preparation:

1. Preheat the oven to 300 degrees. Rub each shank with salt, pepper, and cocoa, and then dredge in 2 tablespoons of flour. Add oil to a large Dutch oven pan or cast-iron skillet and heat on medium-high. Add the shanks and sear on all sides until browned. Remove the shanks and set aside.

2. To the hot pan, add carrots, celery, and onions, stirring carefully to avoid burning, about 5 minutes. Add garlic and stir for another minute, and then deglaze the pan on high with apple cider, Worcestershire, and beef stock. Stir well, scraping the bottom to incorporate all ingredients. Add tomato paste, Kitchen Bouquet, bay leaves, and thyme, stirring until smooth. Return the seared shanks to the pan and spoon the sauce over them. Cover and cook the shanks in the oven for about 2-½ hours until tender but not falling off the bone. Remove the pan from the oven and discard bay leaves.

3. Remove each shank carefully to a platter, keeping the meat intact on the bone. Keep warm. Spoon out the vegetables into a bowl and set aside. To the cooking pan, add ½ cup flour and butter to thicken the sauce, stirring on medium-low heat.

4. To serve, "paint" a spoonful of the Sweet Potato Apple Mash across each plate. Spoon on the cooked vegetables and place the shank — with the bone pointing up — over the mash. Crown the shanks with pan gravy and sprinkle each with lemon zest.

Mashed Sweet Potatoes with Sweet Onions

Ingredients:

- 3 large sweet potatoes, peeled and diced
- 2 medium sweet onions, diced
- 2 tablespoons butter, softened
- ½ tsp nutmeg
- 1 tsp cinnamon
- ½ tsp salt
- ½ tsp black pepper
- ¼ cup half and half

Preparation:

1. Place the sweet potatoes in a saucepan and fill the pan with water to cover. Bring to a boil, reduce heat to medium-low, and simmer for 20 minutes or until potatoes are tender. Remove from the heat, drain, and set aside to cool slightly.
2. In a saucepan, melt butter over low heat. Add the diced onion and simmer for 5 minutes or until the onions are tender.
3. In a large bowl, mash the potatoes thoroughly with the seasonings and the half and half, then stir in the onions with a fork until combined.

Suggested Accompaniment:

- **Cabernet Sauvignon:** Rowland Cellars Cenay (Napa Valley, California)
- **Zinfandel:** Campus Oaks (California)

Braised Wild Boar Shanks

Swirling Spots and Tideflat Trout

As we discussed my dad's upcoming visit, I suggested that we do some in-shore fishing for Speckled Trout and Spot-tailed Bass on the tide flats at the outflow of the Ogeechee River into St. Catherine's Sound with my friend and neighbor Kevin.

When the day finally arrived, Dad, Kevin and I drove to the Kilkenny Marina and were quickly on our way down Kilkenny Creek to the Ogeechee.

As we approached the saw grass along the shore, Kevin cut the engines and raised the props out of the water. "It's high tide, but we've only got about two feet of water, and as soon as the tide starts heading out, we'll  have to move quickly or get stuck!" Although the water in the tide flats is constantly churning and muddy, Kevin assured us that we'd be able to see the tails of the bass as they searched, nose down, for crabs and snails.

Both the bass and trout also feed on shrimp and small fish, so by using shrimp- and minnow-imitating flies, our strategy would be effective on either species.

As we approached a small tip of land jutting out of the grass, Dad saw a small bunch of tailing reds near an oyster bed on the far side of the point.

Dad laid his silver menhaden imitator fly softly onto the water's surface about ten feet to the left of the school. A long second later, the water exploded where the fly had been, and Dad reared back to expertly set the hook on the fleeing fish. It wasn't big, but playing it on a six-weight fly rod made it a challenge!

A short time later, Dad led the fish into Kevin's waiting hands. Kevin raised the fish out of the water and slipped the hook out of its mouth. "About four pounds, Don! Not bad for our first fish," he said as he released it into the murky water.

We were soon casting back toward the oyster bed again as Kevin poled us beyond the point. A small pool hugged the bank about fifty yards ahead, and I cast my fly toward the near bank as Kevin maneuvered the boat.

"Fish On!" I shouted as an unseen predator smacked my shrimp-imitating fly. When it realized that it was hooked, the fish made a run straight for the marsh grass, hoping to break free. I expected it to do exactly that, though, and turned it back to open water.

"That's a nice trout!" Kevin said. "He won't run as much as a Spot but keep a tight line on him. Trout have hard mouths, so it's harder to set the hook on them."

Following his advice, I soon boated the feisty silver fish. It was eighteen inches long and almost three pounds. "Let's keep that one. He's a perfect size for eating," Kevin said as I removed the hook and dropped the fish into the ice chest.

When we reached the end of the pool, Dad and I reeled in. The tide was receding, and we needed to get to deeper water without delay.

As we reached the bay, Kevin swung the nose of the boat down a reedy shore.

"There's a huge bull Spot rolling on the surface dead ahead," Kevin shouted as we coasted toward a swirl in the water. "One of you needs to get a fly in his face – NOW!" Dad was near the bow, so he stepped onto the casting deck and quickly flicked the fly toward the big fish. Nothing. He stripped the line back toward the boat and flicked it again – this time a little further in front of the fish.

"Jerk it hard a couple of times!" Kevin urged. "We need to get his attention!" The water splashed as the fly smacked the surface.

The fish lunged and grabbed the fly, and Dad raised his rod tip to set the hook. The fight was on! The fish raced away from the boat toward deeper water, Dad's reel singing as line peeled away. He had been in battles like this before with bonefish, permits, barracuda and amber jacks, and he was able to deftly apply enough pressure to turn the bronze beast back toward the boat.

A couple of runs and retrieves later, the line suddenly went slack. "He spit the hook!" Dad said, disappointed as he reeled in the remaining line. Upon inspecting the fly, however, it quickly became clear what had happened: the weight and strength of the fish had been enough to straighten the hook! "That must have been a pretty good-sized fish!" Dad said. "My guess is that he was at least thirty-five pounds," Kevin replied.

A short time later, as he cut the engines and we drifted toward an old jetty, Kevin suggested that Dad cast his fly along the edge of the rocks while I switched to live shrimp and ply shallow pockets between some pilings that extended into the channel from the jetty.

A few casts later, Dad and I both hooked up – Dad with a Trout and me with a nice Spot. We each played our fish until they tired. "Can we keep this Red?" I asked, seeing that my fish was a legal twenty-five inches. "I've never eaten a Spot, but I've heard they're excellent."

By this time, the sun was sinking toward the western horizon, and the wind had begun to pick up, so Dad decided that it was time to call it a day. We had boated seventeen fish, keeping two Trout and two Reds. We normally practice catch-and-release, but having never tasted either Specs or Reds, we decided that keeping a couple of each species would not put a dent in their robust populations.

As we stowed our gear for the short boat ride to the marina, I asked Dad if he had enjoyed this trip as much as our previous trip for Striped Bass. "They were both great," he replied, "but it's hard to beat that 'swirlin' Spot and tide flat Trout!"

Artichoke Hearts Salad

Dressing Ingredients:

- ¼ cup lemon juice
- 2 tsp Dijon mustard
- 1 Tbsp Pomegranate-infused balsamic vinegar
- 1 garlic clove, minced
- Kosher salt & coarsely ground black pepper – to taste
- 1¼ cups extra virgin olive oil
- 1 Tbsp fresh basil leaves, chopped

Dressing Preparation:

1. Combine all of the ingredients except the oil and basil together in a medium mixing bowl. Slowly whisk in the oil, and add the basil leaves just before serving.

Salad Ingredients:

- 2 cups mixed baby garden greens
- 1 cup fresh kale, chopped
- 1 cup artichoke hearts, coarsely chopped
- ¼ cup kalamata olives, pitted and chopped
- ¼ cup reggiano-asiago cheese, shaved

Salad Preparation:

1. In a large salad bowl, combine the mixed greens, kale, artichoke hearts and olives. Toss.
2. Add the basil to the dressing, then add 2 to 3 Tbsp of the dressing and toss again. Add more dressing to taste.
3. Spoon the salad onto salad plates and top with the shaved cheese. Serve immediately.

Basil & Garlic Marinated Spot-tail Bass

Ingredients:

- 1 cup chopped basic leaves
- 3 garlic cloves, minced
- ¼ cup white balsamic vinegar
- ¼ cup low-sodium vegetable juice
- 1 tsp blackened seasoning
- ½ tsp sea salt
- ½ tsp coarsely ground black pepper
- Four 4 to 6 ounce bass fillets (about 1 pound)
- 2 Tbsp extra virgin olive oil

Preparation:

1. In a shallow glass loaf pan, combine the first seven ingredients and blend thoroughly.
2. Pat the fillets dry, then place them in the load pan. Swirl and turn to coat each piece completely. Cover and marinate in the refrigerator for 1 hour.
3. In a large sauté pan, heat the oil over medium-high heat until shimmering. Remove the fillets from the marinade to the pan and cook for 4 to 5 minutes on each side or until fish flakes easily with a fork.
4. Transfer the fillets to a platter and serve.

* Grouper, Snapper and Tilapia are acceptable alternatives.

Ogeechee Red Rice

Ingredients:

- ¼ lb thick-cut smoky bacon
- 1 cup diced yellow onion
- ¼ cup each diced green and red bell peppers
- 1 Tbsp celery seed
- 1 tsp chicken soup base
- 3 cups diced and seeded Roma tomatoes
- 2 cups tomato sauce
- 1 cup medium grain white rice

Preparation:

1. Saute the bacon, onions and green peppers in a large, oven-proof stock pot until the bacon is slightly crispy and the vegetables are tender.
2. Pre-heat the oven to 300 degrees F.
3. Add the celery seed, soup base, tomatoes and tomato sauce and bring the mixture to a boil.
4. Add the rice and mix thoroughly.
5. Bake for 15 minutes, stir thoroughly, then bake for another 15-20 minutes. Remove from the oven to cool slightly before serving.

Suggested Accompaniment:

- **Rose of Pinot Noir:** Toad Hollow (California)
- **Beer:** Third Shift Amber Lager

Basil & Garlic Marinated Spot-tail Bass

Dancing with Bill's Bass

Most residents of the town in which we lived following our relocation from Seattle don't know it, but it is an established destination for professional fishing celebrities. In 2001, Flip Pallot, an outdoor television personality, featured fly-fishing for bass and crappie at The Ford Plantation on his show. More recently, Bill Dance, a former Bass Masters professional circuit fisherman turned television show host, lent his name and technical expertise to help develop the Grand Lagoon at WaterWays Township.

Both The Ford Plantation and WaterWays Township are private, gated communities, so I felt extremely lucky to be offered the opportunity to fish the Grand Lagoon with my friend David. This lake is, for the most part, man-made; it was developed by Dance's team to support a robust population of trophy large-mouth bass, bream, and crappie.

As it evolved over the first few years, the lagoon proved to be a great habitat for the bass – almost too good, in fact. Dance's team biologists determined that the population of small to medium sized bass was too healthy, and that they were eating the large fish out of house and home and needed to be reduced in number.

Enter David and Stan. David's real estate agent mentioned that he worked with the WaterWays Township real estate sale team, and had recommended him to help with the culling process (and have a little fun in the process!). David invited me to come along and by good fortune we were able to pick up some local knowledge about the best lures and locations from the lake's biologist.

Bass fishing tends to slacken during the winter months, so our expectations of catching a monster weren't all that high when we set out on our first junket. It was 55°, and the surface water temperature was around 52°, so we knew that the fish would be schooled up – at least until sundown. Our depth finder helped us find a couple of schools of good-sized fish, so we anchored the boat and grabbed our rods.

"Bass will usually go after worms no matter what the water temperature is," David said. "After you cast it, let it sink to the bottom, then slowly retrieve it by raising your rod tip two to three feet, reeling a little as you go," he coached. He had rigged his favorite plastic worm – a six-inch dark blue beast – and cast to another area.

It was comfortably cool as the sun dropped in the western sky. We made our way up the shoreline, casting our baits into shady pockets in the cattails and under wax myrtle branches hanging out over the water. The fish didn't seem to be in the mood to feed, but finally David said, "There he is!" And he reared back to set the hook on a fish. After a short but energetic tussle, which included an aerobatic leap and wiggle characteristic of largemouth bass– a nice fourteen incher.

"Let's see now, we bet ten bucks on who would catch the first fish, right?" David joked.

"No way!" I exclaimed. "You've out-fished me every time we've gone and I've never fished with a worm, so why would I make a silly bet like that?" "Well, it was worth a try," he replied, laughing, as he unhooked his fish and dropped it into the ice chest.

It didn't take long before I felt a subtle tug on my line, so I raised the rod tip. Sure enough, a nice bass had grabbed my worm and headed away from the boat. After a couple of energetic runs and jumps, though, it shook the hook and was gone. "Darn it!" I exclaimed as I brought the worm into the boat to re-hook it. "You can't always count on them hooking themselves. Give it a quick, hard pull just to make sure it's hooked next time," David said.

Doing my best to follow his advice, I was able to hook and bring another acrobatic fish into the boat about a half hour later. The fish was a robust 14 inches, so I dropped him into the ice chest. The afternoon sun continued toward the horizon with a gentle breeze that threatened to become chilly. Our depth finder showed several schools of fish, but they weren't acting interested in the easy meal we offered them.

"I guess we'll have to wait until it gets close to dark before they start feeding," David said, taking a sip of his warm coffee. After a short lull, David shouted, "There you are!" and reared back on his rod. "Gotcha!" I also felt a gentle pull on my line, so I set the hook and began playing a feisty fish. Paying close attention to our respective fish, neither David nor I were able to tell how big the others' fish was, so we were pleasantly surprised when both fish launched themselves into the air and we saw that they were both two-plus pounders.

As both bass wriggled wildly across the top of the water, I thought about an energetic routine my daughter's dance class had done at a recital many years before, and couldn't help but say, "I guess we're dancin' with Bill's bass now!" We both laughed, as we played the fish to the boat.

"Rainbow" Deviled Eggs w/Vidalia Onion Ribbons

Ingredients:

- **Hard-Boiled Eggs**
- 6 large eggs
- 3 quarts of water, divided
- **Colored Egg Whites**
- 4 tablespoons white vinegar, divided
- 2 drops each of red, blue, green, and yellow food coloring
- **Deviled Eggs**
- 2 tablespoons low-fat mayonnaise
- 2 tablespoons no-fat sour cream
- 1½ tablespoons (+ more to taste) horseradish mustard
- Coarsely-ground black pepper
- Kosher salt
- ½ teaspoon smoked paprika
- 3 tablespoons green Vidalia Onion tops, sliced diagonally into thin ringlets
- ½ cup extra virgin olive oil

Preparation:

1. Pour 1½ quarts water in a 3-quart pan and bring to a boil. Gently place eggs into boiling water and let cook for 10 minutes; remove pan from burner.
2. Pour 3 cups cold water into a large bowl. Remove eggs from pan and into the cold water; let sit until completely cooled.
3. Peel and then halve the eggs lengthwise and spoon yolks into a separate bowl, reserving egg whites.

1. Spoon 1 tablespoons vinegar and 1 cup cold water into each of 4 small bowls or large coffee mugs; drip 2 drops of each food coloring into each bowl or mug.
2. Gently place 3 egg white halves into each bowl or mug; let stand for 1 to 3 hours.

1. Remove egg white halves, drain gently (do not dry) and place on deviled egg plate.
2. Blend the mayonnaise, sour cream, and mustard with the egg yolks until smooth. Season with pepper and salt to taste. Spoon a heaping tsp of mixture into each egg white half. Sprinkle each with smoked paprika and top with the green onion ringlets.

Blackened Largemouth Bass Filets

Ingredients:

- 6-8 two ounce bass filets
- 4 tablespoons blackened seasoning
- Non-stick cooking spray
- 2 tablespoons Canola oil

Preparation:

1. Spray a 9" saute pan with non-stick cooking spray, then heat the oil to shimmering over medium-high heat.
2. Pat filets dry and spoon seasoning into a shallow bowl. Dredge each filet in seasoning and place them gently into the hot oil; cook 3-4 minutes on each side until flesh is opaque and flakes with a fork. Remove to a platter and cover loosely with foil.

Yellow Rice w/Baby Vidalia Onion Greens

Ingredients:

- 1 cup Yellow [Vigo] Rice
- 2 cups water
- ½ cup baby Vidalia onions, sliced cross-wise into ¼" rounds; separate the white and green pieces*
- Kosher salt
- Coarsely ground black pepper

Preparation:

1. Prepare the rice according to directions. (Note: Yellow Rice typically requires 35-40 minutes cooking time, so plan accordingly.)
2. Melt the EVOO over medium-high heat in a small saute pan. Saute the white onion pieces, stirring frequently, until opaque and soft. Turn the heat to low.
3. 5 minutes before the rice is done, stir in the green onion pieces and cook, stirring until the rice is ready. Season lightly with salt and pepper.
4. Drain the rice and spoon into a serving bowl and mix in the onions.

* ¼ cup of chopped green peppers can be substituted for the green onion slices.

Broiled Carrots and Asparagus

Ingredients:

- ½ lb small carrots, washed and rinsed, with green tops removed except for 1"
- ½ lb fresh asparagus, rinsed and washed, with woody stems removed
- 3 tablespoons Extra Virgin Olive Oil
- 1 ½ tablespoons granulated garlic
- Coarsely ground fresh pepper

Preparation:

1. Pre-heat the broiler and grill.
2. Pour the EVOO into a flat, shallow bowl; swish the carrots and asparagus in oil until lightly coated.
3. Place the carrots on the grill and roll gently to sear; sprinkle generously with garlic, then return to broiler and cook for 4 minutes.
4. Turn the carrots, add the asparagus to the grill; sprinkle both with garlic then return to broiler and cook for 4 minutes.
5. Remove to platter and serve.

Suggested Accompaniment

- **Chardonnay:** St. Michelle Dry Johannesburg Riesling (Columbia Valley, Washington)
- **Beer:** Left Hand Brewery's Milk Stout Nitro (Longmont, Colorado)

Rainbow Deviled Eggs   **Blackened Largemouth Bass Filets**

Broiled Carrots & Asparagus w/Yellow Rice

Poppin' Pigs on Cedar Knoll

After sharing stories about feral pig hunting at a hunting camp near Estill, South Carolina with several work colleagues, two of them coming to town for a company sales meeting decided that they wanted to hunt there with me. A few phone calls and emails later, we devised a plan and I contacted Cedar Knoll Plantation to book our visit. This would be my third visit, and Hayward, the owner/proprietor, was happy to hear from me.

Geoff, one of my colleagues, owned his own plane and had flown it from his home in Pennsyvania to Savannah for the sales meeting, and after the meeting wrapped up and we met to discuss our hunt, Geoff told me that he and Sherman, the other colleague, had decided to fly to Estill and meet me there. The next morning, I headed out for a fairly short 90 minute drive to Cedar Knoll.

Hayward met Geoff and Sherman at the nearby airport and brought them back to camp, arriving within minutes of me. I quickly unloaded my gear. Sherman had chosen to borrow my .30—06 bolt action rifle rather than having to deal with the airlines to bring his own gun from his home in Texas; I would use my trusty .243 bolt action. Geoff had a .300 Win Mag semi-automatic.

Once they had unloaded their gear from Hayward's truck, we all headed up to the nearby gun range to make sure that our guns were all properly sighted in. A half-hour later, we were back at the lodge for lunch. After eating the filling meal, I knew that our biggest challenge for the afternoon 'sit' would be to avoid dozing off!

Bellies filled, we donned our hunting gear and grabbed our knapsacks filled with water, candy bars, binoculars and flashlights. We climbed into Hayward's pickup and settled in for the half-hour ride to a hunting area called "The Jungle" because of its dense undergrowth and old-growth live oaks. The Jungle was my favorite of the area, and I wondered where Hayward planned to drop each of us.

"I think a stand you haven't seen before will work well this afternoon," Hayward said to me. "I've seen a lot of sign, so we've been dropping corn every other day." Sherman piped up, responding "Dibs!" From Dallas, Sherman was an avid pig hunter, while Geoff had never hunted them.

"OK!" Hayward chuckled at Sherman's quick claim. "We'll put Geoff on the field stand," referring to an open area with a small pond about 125 yards from the stand. "Even though it's winter, it's been pretty dry, so they've been coming in to drink nearly every day."

"Sounds good to me!" Geoff replied enthusiastically. "It's 2:30 now; what time do you think they'll come in?" he asked.

"About a half hour before dark – which will be about 4:30," Hayward answered.

As we dropped Sherman off at his stand, we could hear the rumble of the diesel dump truck Hayward's property manager, Billy, was driving behind us. About a hundred yards from the stand, Billy began dropping corn from the back of the truck, continuing to about forty yards short of the stand, then continuing about twenty-five yards on the opposite side of the stand.

"The sound of the truck is like a dinner bell!" Hayward said. "I hope that Sherman gets into his stand before they come running." We would learn later that he wasn't kidding!

Geoff was next, with Billy repeating the baiting procedure behind us. Having heard Hayward's comment about getting into the stand quickly, Geoff was already climbing the ladder to the box blind at the top of a twenty foot tower as Hayward and I pulled away.

The stand that Hayward had chosen for me was at the top of a "T," so I would have three shooting lanes to watch. Given the increased odds of three lanes versus two, I was happy with Hayward's choice.

As I quickly climbed into my stand while Billy dropped corn, I heard a rifle shot in the distance. Based on the volume, I guessed that Sherman had taken a shot!

Almost before I settled into my chair, I saw two jet-black pigs – identical twin boars I guessed would weigh about 150 pounds each – galloping up the road toward the corn. Hayward wasn't kidding! The sound of the diesel was a dinner bell, and the pigs were apparently hungry.

While I was happy that the pigs had appeared, it made for a dilemma, knowing that Hayward would not be back to pick us up for two and a half hours! So I settled in to watch the pigs in front of me and hope that something bigger showed up before they had their fill and decided to leave.

About thirty minutes had passed when I heard another gunshot from the direction of Geoff's stand. The pigs feeding in front of me definitely heard it too, and they began to fidget nervously, trying to decide whether to continuing eating or run into the underbrush.

Sensing that they were thinking about leaving, I raised my gun to my shoulder and centered one of the pigs in my rifle scope crosshairs. He had begun to settle down a little as he resumed eating, but I decided that he was nervous enough that he could leave at any moment.

Even though I had decided to shoot, a new dilemma arose because the pigs were eating side-by-side: if I shot one, there was a pretty good chance that the shot would kill them both! If I was hunting public land, or on my hunting club lease, I wouldn't hesitate to shoot both pigs. Here, however, Hayward's rule was that each hunter could only take one pig per day or pay $300 per additional hog! So I waited for them to separate enough for a clean shot.

Finally, the back pig lifted his head and turned back down the road. I knew that the front pig would likely follow, so I pulled the trigger before he could make a move.

The gun barked and the pig dropped in its tracks. We wouldn't have to track him into the undergrowth – that was for sure!

I settled back in my chair to wait for Hayward to return; he didn't want hunters to climb out of their stand before he picked them up, both to avoid spreading scent and for safety's sake. Checking my watch, I was relieved to find that it would only be another hour or so before pickup.

When the truck arrived to retrieve me and my pig, I quickly saw that Sherman had also shot a nice black pig, but that Geoff was not in the truck.

"Where's Geoff?" I asked.

"He and Billy are tracking his pig," Hayward replied. "We'll go back to help, if they haven't already found it."

When we rolled up to the meadow in front of Geoff's stand, we saw a flashlight waving to us from the edge of the woods, and Hayward drove to where Billy was standing.

"We've found plenty of sign, so we're pretty sure we'll find it soon, but we don't want to leave it overnight for the coyotes to chew on!" Billy said as we climbed out of the truck. Hayward, Sherman and I grabbed our flashlights and headed into the undergrowth behind Billy. Only a few minutes had passed, though, when Geoff shouted "Over here!"

We quickly dragged his spotted boar out of the woods, tossed it in the bed of the truck with Sherman's and my pig, and headed toward the lodge.

"You boys sure popped some nice pigs tonight!" Hayward said as we unloaded our game at the processing shed. "Poppin' Pigs on Cedar Knoll" had a nice ring to it!

Tossed Romaine w/White Balsamic Vinaigrette

Ingredients:

- 2 cups shredded romaine lettuce leaves
- ¼ cup extra virgin olive oil
- 3 Tbsp white balsamic vinegar
- 1 tsp sugar
- Kosher salt, to taste
- Freshly ground black pepper, to taste
- 2 hard-boiled eggs, sliced thinly into discs

Preparation:

1. Place the lettuce in a salad bowl.
2. In a small, non-reactive mixing bowl, combine the next four ingredients and mix thoroughly.
3. Pour the vinaigrette over the lettuce leaves, add the salt and pepper to taste, and toss to coat.
4. Place the hard-boiled egg discs atop the salad and serve.

Crispy Cashew Rice

Ingredients:

- 3 cups low sodium chicken broth
- 1½ cups long grain white rice
- ½ cup cashews, chopped
- ¼ cup green onions, chopped
- Vegetable spray
- Kosher salt and coarsely ground black pepper, to taste

Preparation:

1. In a 2 qt pot, bring the broth to a boil over high heat.
2. Add the rice, then cover the pot and reduce the heat to low. Simmer for 30-35 minutes until all of the liquid has been absorbed.
3. Add the chopped cashews and green onions, then spread the rice evenly on a 9" × 12" (or similar sized) sheet pan. Let cool to room temperature.
4. Move the rice to a 12" saute pan lightly coated with vegetable spray over medium heat. Being careful not to burn the rice, turn it over in sections with a spatula. When it has acquired a thin light brown crust, remove to a platter and serve.

Roast Wild Boar w/Sage & Honey

Ingredients:

- 3 lbs wild boar shoulder
- ⅓ cup of olive oil
- The juice of an orange
- 1 tablespoon wine vinegar
- 1 tablespoon mild mustard
- 1 – 2 tablespoon thyme honey
- 2 cloves of garlic, pounded
- 1 tablespoon dried sage (pounded)
- ½ teaspoon of red hot ground chilli.
- 1 teaspoon dried thyme
- 1 teaspoon rosemary
- 1 tablespoon oregano
- 2 bay leaves
- Salt
- Freshly ground variety of many peppers
- Peeled potatoes, cut in two or four pieces (I prefer small whole ones)
- 3 medium size onions cut in four
- 2 tomatoes, peeled and cut into small slices

Preparation:

1. Preheat the oven to 300°F.
2. Wash the meat and let it drain in a colander.
3. Pound the garlic and rub the meat. Add the mustard and the honey and sprinkle with salt, pepper and chili.
4. Put it in a bowl and add the orange juice, olive oil and vinegar, as well as the bay leaves, pound sage, rosemary, thyme and oregano. Reserve some of the four last ingredients to season the potatoes.
5. Marinate for 2 – 3 hours in the refrigerator.
6. Preheat the oven to 200 degrees C.
7. Peel, wash and cut potatoes, if needed and pierce all the small ones with a sharp knife so that the steam will penetrate through and cut the bigger ones in two or four pieces.
8. Put them in a bowl and sprinkle with salt, pepper and the four ingredients we reserved (thyme, rosemary, sage and oregano).
9. Put the meat in your roasting pan and place the potatoes around the meat. Cut the onions and peeled tomatoes into small slices.
10. Add the leftover marinade and cover it with the parchment paper and aluminum foil and cover the tin air tight.
11. Place tin near the centre of oven and reduce temperature to 180o C and roast for about 2 – 2 ½ hours.
12. Remove the aluminum tent and continue baking for another half an hour or until the meat and potatoes is golden on top.

Zucchini & Tomatoes with Anchovy Sauce

Ingredients:

- 3 Tbsp extra virgin olive oil, divided
- 1 cup fresh zucchini, sliced cross-wise
- 3 garlic cloves, sliced thinly
- 1 tsp anchovy paste
- 2 Tbsp capers
- 1 cup heirloom tomatoes, cut into 1" cubes
- Freshly Ground Black Pepper – to taste

Preparation:

1. In 12" saute pan, heat 2 Tbsp of the oil over medium high till shimmering. Add the zucchini slices and saute on each side for about 2 minutes. Remove to a side plate.
2. Add the remaining oil, then add the garlic and the anchovy paste. Stir to integrate the paste into the oil as the garlic releases its fragrance. Saute for another 3-4 minutes then stir in the capers.
3. Add the tomatoes to the sauce and stir to coat thoroughly. Return the zucchini to the pan and add pepper and salt, to taste. Toss to integrate the ingredients.
4. Transfer to a serving bowl and serve.

Suggested Accompaniment:

- **Beer:** Ice-Cold Dos Equis with a lime wedge
- **Pinot Grigio:** Monte Maria – Chile

Roast Wild Boar w/Sage and Honey

Offshore at the Outer Banks

After moving to Virginia in April 2015, it didn't take long for me to start missing the fishing opportunities I had enjoyed in the Savannah, Georgia area, so I was very happy to get a phone call one late February day asking me if I wanted to join a group of co-workers on an offshore fishing trip in mid-March. March is a little early, even for the south, to think about offshore fishing, but the colleague who was setting everything up had spoken with the charter boat 'skipper' about weather and how fishing was going in the area. Good news on both fronts (although we all know that weather can turn on a dime!), so a group of six of us began preparations for the six-hour drive from Manassas, Virginia to Nag's Head, North Carolina.

By six that evening, we had all arrived at the hotel near the docks and met at a local restaurant for dinner. We enjoyed our meal and chatted happily about the impending excursion. The weather was forecast to be cool but fair, with a light breeze out of the northwest, so we retired early to dreams of the day ahead.

Being used to boarding an hour before dawn when I was salmon fishing off the Washington coast, I was ready as the dawn began to paint the eastern sky with a beautiful yellow brush. An hour before dawn wasn't the plan in this case, though: Captain Brian and first mate Jeff arrived at the boat about a half hour later than I expected, but still earlier than the rest of our party! The group included Janine and her husband Jim, Steve (a retired Air Force colonel) and his son Robert, "Pepe" (a retired army helicopter pilot), and me. Everyone had sworn that they were veterans of offshore fishing, so the calm weather promised an uneventful day on the Atlantic.

The run from the docks to the fishing grounds took a little over 90 minutes, and included a couple of choppy areas where the changing tide created a 'rip' in the currents and stirred up some white water as the wind blew against the wave tops. One thing I've learned over the years is that diesel fumes swirling in the back end of any boat can have an unexpected reaction in some people, but we were all surprised when Pepe began feeling nauseous from the fumes and choppy wave action! While we all felt bad for him as he 'chummed' the water with his breakfast, we couldn't help but tease the big, burly combat helicopter pilot for getting seasick in relatively calm water! Unfortunately for him, his symptoms lasted most of the trip, but it never kept him out of the fighting chair when it was his turn to bring in a fish.

When we finally reached the area the captain wanted to fish – a series of underwater mounds that rose from the sea floor to about a hundred feet from the surface – the currents and wave action churned against these mounds, creating a virtual smorgasbord for predatory fish.

Jeff had everything ready when Brian shouted back to him to drop the baits into the water. We would be fishing with 'skirted' ballyhoo trolled at various distances behind the boat. While Brian had told us to expect mostly blackfin tuna, he allowed as how we might also encounter wahoo, big-eye tuna, small yellowfin tuna and albacore.

After we drew numbered slips from Steve's hat, the order would be Janine, Steve, me, Robert, Pepe and Jim. So, not more than two or three minutes after the baits were set, the first rod bent with its reel screaming as a fish tore away from the boat. Janine got settled in the fighting chair and Jeff positioned the rod butt into the holder in the chair, allowing Janine to fight the fish without having to hang onto the rod for dear life! This first fish was more of a fighter than anyone expected, and after a couple of runs back and forth across the back of the boat, the rod went slack.

"I'm pretty sure that was a fairly big wahoo!" Brian shouted to us and we helped Jeff get the lines back in the water and re-bait the rod Janine had just used. The baits were re-set as we resumed our troll, and I could hear Brian tell Jeff that he was 'marking' fish on his sonar.

No sooner had he said it, another rod bent sharply and Steve jumped into the fighting chair as the rest of us (except Pepe!) reeled in the other baits to prevent tangles. Steve showed us that he had, indeed, fished offshore before as he deftly fought a nice blackfin tuna to the back of the boat for Jeff to gaff.

"Great job!" Brian called back to Steve as Jeff dropped the fish into the fish box full of ice. This time, I watched Jeff carefully as he re-baited the hooks, figuring that I could help him if we got into a lot of fish.

Sure enough, about an hour (and five fat blackfins) later, three reels screamed simultaneously. We put Pepe in the fighting chair while Robert and I each fought our fish from rod-holder positions on the railings. Jim, Steve and Janine quickly reeled in the other baits as Jeff and Brian coached each of us fighting fish to keep them from crossing lines. We lost one of the three fish, but soon boated the other two, after which I grabbed a ballyhoo and baited the hooks.

"Hey," Jeff said, seeing me baiting a line, "are you trying to put me out of a job?"

"Not at all," I replied. "I figure that the more quickly we can get all of the lines back in the water, the MORE work you'll have to do!"

'Okay, okay," he said, smiling. "You make a good point!"

As the morning wore on and the 'bite' slowed considerably, Brian decided that we should try dropping jig baits near the top of one of the mounds. "There are fish showing on my sonar just above the mounds, so we should be able to catch a few."

Sure enough, we hooked two feisty albacore (and one blue shark!) within a few minutes, and followed them with one more awhile later.

"I expected to do a little better," Brian said, "but we have about twenty fish in the box and the breeze is starting to pick up. Unless someone objects, I'd like to get us back to the dock before we have to fight our way in!"

No one argued, so we reeled in the lines and helped Jeff stow the rods for the run in. It took a little over two hours, owing to the wind and wave action that we didn't have outbound, but everyone enjoyed the salt air, the seagulls and the afternoon sun in our faces.

Once on the dock, we figured that Brian had probably been keeping closer tabs on the fish count than he had let on, because we wound up with twenty beautiful fish after a great day offshore at the Outer Banks!

Seared Blackfin Tuna Loin

Ingredients:

Tuna Steaks

- 6 to 8 1 oz tuna loin medallions
- Kosher salt
- Freshly ground black pepper
- 2 Tbsp black sesame seeds
- 2 Tbsp white sesame seeds
- 1 tbsp sunflower oil

Preparation:

1. Season tuna steaks all over with salt and pepper. Combine black and white sesame seeds on a shallow plate, then gently press tuna steaks into seeds to coat them on all sides.
2. In a medium skillet over medium-high heat, heat oil until hot. Add tuna steaks to the pan and sear 30 seconds to 1 minute per side, depending on desired doneness. Transfer to a cutting board.

Gingered Sticky Rice

Ingredients:

- 2 cups white rice
- 3 ½ cups water
- 1 Tbsp grated ginger
- ¾ tsp Kosher salt

Preparation:

1. In a 2 qt. pot, soak the rice in the water for 1 hour prior to cooking.
2. Stir in the salt.
3. Place the pot over high heat and bring the water to a boil. Reduce the heat to medium low and cover the pot, leaving the lid slightly off on one side to vent. Stir in the ginger and cook for 10 minutes, but DO NOT stir the rice while cooking.
4. After 10 minutes, check to see if all of the water has been absorbed by gently pulling back the rice from the center of the pot. If any water remains, continue cooking until it has been absorbed, but do not let it overcook.
5. Remove the pot from the heat and cover completely, then let it stand for 10 minutes before transferring the rice to a bowl for serving.

Carrot & Jicama Slaw

Ingredients:

- 4 medium carrots, peeled and shredded
- 1 cup jicama, washed, rinsed and shredded
- 2 large garlic cloves, minced
- Zest and juice of 1 lemon
- ¼ tsp Kosher salt
- ½ tsp coarsely ground black pepper
- 1 tsp brown sugar
- ½ tsp apple cider vinegar
- 2 Tbsp olive oil

Preparation:

1. In a large, non-reactive mixing bowl, toss together the carrots, jicama, garlic, lemon zest & juice, salt, pepper, and brown sugar. Let stand for at least 30 minutes.
2. Stir in the vinegar and olive oil.
3. Taste and add more salt, pepper and/or sugar, if desired.
4. Refrigerate in a non-reactive, airtight container until ready to serve.

Suggested Accompaniment:

- **Sauvignon Blanc:** Leese-Fitch (Napa Valley, California)
- **Beer:** Ice-Cold Pyramid Hefeweizen Ale (with an orange wedge)

Gingered Sticky Rice   **Carrot & Jicama Slaw**
Seared Blackfin Tuna Loin

Little Boys and Big Bream

Although I had caught sunfish and perch visiting my grandparents in Iowa when I was about 10, Bream (pronounced "Brim") were unknown to me when we moved from Seattle to Savannah. So it was fortuitous that I met David, a retired ATF agent married to a woman with whom I worked. David loves to fish, having almost joined the professional bass fishing tour in the 1980s. A by-product of doing a lot of bass fishing, especially if you have kids or grand kids, is fishing for Bream and Crappie.

One particularly mild winter (when the weather reminded me of summer in Seattle!), I talked with David about going Bass and Bream fishing. His answer was welcome: he had been offered access to a private lake near our homes, and I soon convinced him that we needed to go fish that lake, even though he had been told that it was heavily populated with Gizzard Shad, a non-edible species of fish that preys on the young of other fish. David was concerned that there wouldn't be a lot of Bass or Bream if the rumor about the Shad was true.

Figuring that we could probably catch (and release!) Shad if there weren't many game fish, we forged ahead with our plan to visit the lake the next week. Saturday morning, however, he called me with a slight change of plans: his two grandsons would be coming that afternoon to visit for a week while their parents attended a work conference in Atlanta. The boys were five and seven, and would love to go fishing with us, but were young enough to be a handful! I assured David that I didn't mind if they came along, and that I would do my best to keep them busy while he managed the boat and their fishing poles.

Sunday dawned clear and warm, with barely a breath of wind. I was looking forward to meeting the boys – Jackson and James. They were shy at first, but by the time we got to the bait shop to pick up some live crickets, they were chattering away like a couple of squirrels.

"Are you going to put the crickets on our hooks, Big Daddy?" Jackson asked David. "Either I will or Mr. Stan will – unless YOU want to do it yourself!" he answered. "No way!" Jackson fairly shrieked. Apparently, the idea of putting a hook through their bodies didn't sound like a good idea, even for a seven year old!

We arrived at the lake shortly after noon and were happy to see that there were no other boats on the water. David's friend had suggested that we try a couple of different spots, so once we had the boat in the water and our gear loaded, I helped David strap life jackets on the boys and get them situated on the center seat.

As we made our way toward a far corner of the lake with lots of underbrush hanging out over the water, I got the boys' hooks baited and ready to drop into the water. David had suggested that we start out by letting the boys each catch a fish before wetting our own lines. Remembering how excited my son Luke had been catching his first fish, I certainly couldn't object, even though this wasn't their first fishing trip.

Mere seconds had passed from the baits hitting the water to both rod tips jerking from the pull of Bream on the end of the lines. "I got one, Big Daddy! I got one!" James shouted. "Me, too!" said Jackson. "You don't have it yet!" David replied. "Do you remember how to reel them in?" They both eagerly nodded and began cranking on the handles of their small reels. "Mine's too big!" Jackson shrieked. 'I can't turn the handle!" Almost immediately, he turned and handed his rod to David. "You get him!"

David laughed as he took the rod and began playing the feisty fish. I was keeping a close eye on James, but he was doing well with his fish. "You just tell me if you need any help," I said. "I'm OK," he replied. I wasn't sure, though, if he was having fun or was a little bit scared.

David quickly landed Jackson's fish – a very nice Bream that weighed almost a pound. "You caught a nice fish, Jackson!" I said as David lifted it into the boat. "Big Daddy caught it," he replied. "I helped, but it's your fish," David said. A minute later, James brought his fish to the side of the boat, and I lifted it in for him.

"Another twenty or thirty of these, and we'll be good to go!" David said as I dropped the fish into the cooler. "Twenty or thirty?! We'll be here all week!" I responded. "You and Susan, me and Sally, and the boys – heck, the adults can eat four or five apiece, and the boys will probably eat two each: that's at least twenty-five!" "I can almost guarantee that Susan won't eat more than two," I said, laughing.

After shaking both fish off the hook and into the cooler, I re-baited the boys' lines and handed them each their rod. Jackson immediately turned and handed his to David, who grinned and cast the bobber and cricket toward the bank. James did the same, and we settled in to wait for another bite.

It didn't take long before we had another couple of fish on. James quickly handed his rod to David, imploring 'Big Daddy' to reel it in, while Jackson fought his fish by himself. Another two good-sized Bream went into the cooler, wriggling and flopping as they hit the icy water.

After a while, the bite slowed and David suggested that we move further down the bank to a pocket in the lily pads. "The bottom's a little lighter here, so I'm guessing there's a spawning bed," he said. The water was only four or five feet deep, and we were able to see the darting shadows of fish as they moved from the open area into the thick weeds. David explained that Bream congregate around open beds like this to mate and spawn, then defend the area until the eggs hatch and the babies moved into the safety of the weeds.

Sure enough, the minute our baits hit the water, we could see six or seven fish race out of the weeds to attack. "Their first instinct is to attack intruders, but once they figure out that it's food, it will turn into a feeding frenzy!" David said as he hooked a fish. "A big bed can hold several dozen fish, so if we're lucky we'll be here awhile!"

After their first two each, the boys became bored, so David dug sandwiches and sodas out of his pack and handed them to the antsy kids. "Mr. Stan and I want to catch a few fish before we head home, so you boys eat your lunches, OK?" he asked them. "OK," they both said. "How long will it take?"

Smiling and shaking his head like someone who had heard that question a hundred times, David flung his bait to the far edge of the spawning bed and began twitching it as it settled. Before my bait even hit the water, a fish smacked David's cricket and dove for the weeds. As I watched David set the hook, another fish grabbed my line and headed in the opposite direction. "Do you want to play my fish?" I asked Jackson, who was munching happily on his PB&J sandwich. "No thanks," he said through the sticky mess. I couldn't help but laugh!

By the time the boys finished their meals and began to fidget, David and I had managed to catch enough pudgy Bream for a fish fry. We stowed the rods, hoisted our anchors and headed for the boat ramp.

"How many did we catch, Big Daddy?" James asked David. "I don't know, but maybe Mr. Stan would count them if you asked him nicely," he replied. James asked politely, so I opened the cooler. "You count them with me," I said as I began to lift the fish, one at a time, out of the cooler and into a five gallon plastic bucket I had brought to hold any loose gear. Surprisingly, by the time we had tallied our catch, James had loudly counted out twenty-six of the feisty little critters, most of which were bigger than my outspread hand.

"You little boys sure caught some big Bream!" David said to them as he tousled their hair.

Carrot Slaw

Ingredients:

- 6 medium carrots, peeled and shredded
- 2 large garlic cloves, minced
- Zest and juice of 1 lemon
- ¼ tsp Kosher salt
- ½ tsp coarsely ground black pepper
- 1 tsp brown sugar
- ½ tsp apple cider vinegar
- 2 Tbsp olive oil

Preparation:

1. In a large, non-reactive mixing bowl, toss together the carrots, garlic, lemon zest & juice, salt, pepper, and brown sugar. Let stand for at least 30 minutes.
2. Stir in the vinegar and olive oil.
3. Taste and add more salt, pepper and/or sugar, if desired.
4. Refrigerate in a non-reactive, airtight container until serving.

Oven-Baked WholeBream

Ingredients:

- 6 Bream, cleaned, gilled and scaled, then scored several times
- Canola Oil non-stick spray
- Kosher salt
- Coarsely ground black pepper

Preparation:

1. Preheat the oven to 425 degrees F.
2. Lightly coat a 13" × 19" (or larger) metal cookie sheet with cooking spray.
3. Rinse each Bream under clear, cool water and pat dry.
4. After laying them on the cookie sheet, spray each Bream lightly with cooking spray and season with salt and pepper to taste; flip each fish and repeat.
5. Bake the fish for 20 to 25 minutes, then remove each fish to a platter. Cover loosely with foil until ready to serve.

Southern-Style Baked Beans

Ingredients:

- 2 cups navy or cannelli beans
- ½ lb thick-cut smoky bacon, coarsely chopped
- 1 yellow onion, diced
- 3 Tbsp cane syrup
- 1 tsp kosher salt
- ½ tsp coarsely ground black pepper
- ½ tsp smoked paprika
- ¼ tsp cayenne pepper
- ½ cup ketchup
- 1 Tbsp Worcestershire
- ½ cup (packed) dark brown sugar

Preparation:

1. Soak dried beans overnight in cold water, then simmer soaked beans until tender for 2 hours. Drain, reserving the liquid. Note: If you are using canned beans, omit this step.
2. Preheat oven to 325 degrees F.
3. Place ½ cup of beans in an oven-proof soup pot, then layer in the bacon and onion. Repeat until the beans, bacon and onion are used.
4. Combine the syrup, salt, pepper, mustard, ketchup, Worcestershire sauce and brown sugar in a 2 qt saucepan. Bring the mixture to a boil, then pour it over the bean mixture in the stock pot. Add just enough of the reserved bean water to cover the bean, then cover the pot with a lid or aluminum foil.
5. Bake for 90 minutes, then remove the lid and stir the mixture, adding more bean water as needed to keep the mixture moist and juicy.
6. Bake for another 1½ to 2 hours. Remove from oven and let cool to the temperature desired for serving. (Can also be served cold.)

Savory Cornbread Muffins

Ingredients:

- ½ cup butter, softened
- ⅓ cup white sugar
- ¼ cup agave nectar
- 2 large eggs
- ½ tsp Kosher salt
- 1½ cups all-purpose flour
- ¾ cup cornmeal
- ½ tsp baking powder
- ½ cup buttermilk
- ¾ cup corn kernels

Preparation:

1. Preheat the oven to 400° F.
2. In a large bowl, mix the butter, sugar, agave nectar, eggs and salt together.
3. Stir in the flour, cornmeal and baking powder and blend thoroughly.
4. Stir in the milk and corn kernels.
5. Pour or spoon the batter into prepared muffin cups and bake for 20 to 25 minutes – until a toothpick inserted into the center of a muffin comes out dry.

Suggested Accompaniment:

- **Sauvignon Blanc:** Leese-Fitch (Napa Valley, California)
- **Beer:** Ice-Cold Pyramid Hefeweizen Ale (with an orange wedge)

Oven-Baked Bream

A December Doe

One thing I learned about the South after we moved from Seattle to Savannah was that late-season deer hunting usually isn't the battle with the elements that exists in Washington.

Whether I had to deal with chilly and wet weather from early November through the end of the season and beyond on the west side of the state or drier but usually much colder and frequently snowy conditions on the east side, psyching myself up for the late hunt wasn't always easy!

Late-season deer hunting in southeast Georgia, on the other hand, rarely presents the same challenges: the daytime temperatures only rarely drop below freezing, and rain is almost never a major concern. Add to those differences reasonably accessible hunting places – via an annual permit to hunt Fort Stewart Army Base southwest of Savannah – and relatively low hunting pressure, and you can count me in!

So, when my retired ATF agent friend, David, called to ask what I was planning to do between Christmas and New Year, I suggested that we go deer hunting. The weather was clear and cool – around 40° during the day falling to right around freezing at night. In other words, perfect!

David and I had a pretty good idea where we wanted to go, having visited several excellent areas during the spring turkey season, so when we saw that three of our top areas would be open, we made our plan.

Because of the frequent human and vehicle traffic throughout most areas of the base, the deer – although numerous – were mostly nocturnal, so the very early morning and at last light were really the best times to hunt. And, since the area in which we would be hunting required a drive of over 50 miles and dawn occurred at 5:15 a.m., we agreed that an afternoon hunt would work best for both of us.

The area we selected had a food plot – an area of two or three acres roughly cleared and planted with clovers and winter rye grass that provided much-needed nutrition – within short walking distance of the road. With the temperatures a little lower than usual, we were hopeful that deer would be visiting the food plot on a fairly regular basis.

David and I arrived at our selected hunting area at 3:30, with the temperature around thirty-five degrees under a clear sky. We quietly unloaded our guns and other gear from the back of my station wagon, both glad that we had dressed warmly. While it was only a couple of hours until dark, it can get mighty chilly when you aren't moving around!

We 'tip-toed' (which was quite a sight, what with both of us in our calf-high hunting boots!) up the access road toward the food plot, wondering how much animal traffic there had been. As we broke out of the forest onto the plot, we saw dozens of tracks – some of which were clearly from that morning.

We continued quietly to the far side of the food plot toward a large live oak about a third of the way down the far side of the plot, noting that its outer branches nearly brushed the ground. The wind was negligible, but what there was wafted from the upper corner of the plot toward the oak, so everything to David's right would be up wind.

"Why don't you sit here?" I said quietly to David. "You'll have a full view of the plot, and from the tracks, it looks like the deer are coming out of the upper corner to our left, then angling right in front of you."

"I like it," David said, smiling, as he set up his folding camp chair on the right side of the base of the tree facing the plot. "Where are you going to be?" he asked.

"I'm going to the far corner – to the left of that tree," I replied, pointing to another live oak at the far end of the plot. "That way, we'll have your side of the plot covered, and I can see the lower end behind you."

I walked slowly across the plot, careful to avoid brushing against any grass or plants on which I would leave my scent. About twenty minutes later, I reached the tree and leaned my .243 caliber rifle against it as I set up my chair on the right side of the tree trunk. Checking my sight lines from under the tree, I was pleased with the set-up: with my 8X30 binoculars and 3X9 scope, I would easily be able to see anything that entered the food plot, as well as any game within about fifty yards into the low underbrush on either side of the plot.

David had already settled in, and if he stayed true-to-form with our past excursions, he was probably already noshing quietly on his favorite snack of cheese and crackers, washing it down with grape juice. As I leaned back in my chair, I enjoyed the pure, fresh air and the complete quiet of the woods around us.

The late afternoon ticked by and shooting light began to wane, and I worried that my 'Georgia curse' was still with me.

With only a few minutes of shooting light left, I heard a sound and a whitetail doe suddenly appeared from behind a bush about ten yards from the edge of the plot to my left. She stood without moving for a long thirty seconds or so, eyeing the open ground. Satisfied that no danger was present, she inched a step or two forward, revealing a second, and then more, deer behind her. By the time she reached the edge of the field, I counted seven deer in total, and I was willing to bet that there were more hanging back in the brush. I wasn't going to wait until they all showed themselves, though because I would run out of shooting light.

One by one, they stepped onto the plowed ground and began looking for clover shoots to eat. A couple of the deer were clearly less than a year old, even though they were nearly the same size as the lead doe.

By this time, she was about fifteen to twenty yards into the clearing and well clear of any other animals, so I slowly raised my rifle from my lap to my shoulder and braced it against the trunk of the large oak, then quickly placed the cross-hairs on the doe's shoulder.

The gun kicked and roared as the doe dropped in her tracks. The other deer bolted back toward the underbrush, leaving no opportunity for a shot at another deer. My earlier suspicions were confirmed, however, as I saw three or four deer that hadn't shown themselves join the fleeing herd as they bounded into the forest, white tails waving their departure. I jacked the empty shell out of the chamber and loaded another just in case one of them decided to stop to see what had happened.

The stillness of the forest quickly returned as the last few minutes of light waned. A few minutes later, the soulful hoots of a great horned owl echoed across the plot as I rose from my chair and gathered my gear.

The doe lay where she had fallen, some fifty-five yards from where I had sat. As I reached her and bent to examine the entry wound, I was relieved to see that it's placement was such that she had died without realizing she had been shot. As I knelt beside her, I thanked the forest gods for the opportunity to spend the afternoon in such majestic surroundings, and to have had the opportunity to harvest such a beautiful animal.

David carried my chair and rifle as I dragged the doe across the plot toward the car. By this time, it was essentially pitch black and the temperature had dropped to near freezing, so I gave David the keys and suggested that he go ahead of me and start the engine – and fire up the heater!

Congratulating me as we loaded the deer into the back of the station wagon, David chuckled "Well, I guess you broke the curse and got yourself a 'December Doe!'"

Arugula w/Sliced Plums, Walnuts & Raspberry Balsamic Vinegar

Ingredients:

- 2 cups fresh Arugula leaves, washed and patted dry
- ½ cup shredded carrots
- 1 small red onion, sliced thinly
- 2 Bosc pears, washed, cored and sliced lengthwise into eighths
- ¼ cup chopped walnuts
- 3 Tbsp raspberry balsamic vinegar

Preparation:

1. Toss the Arugula leaves, carrots, onion and plums together in a medium salad bowl.
2. Sprinkle on the chopped walnuts, drizzle with the vinegar and toss gently to mix thoroughly, then serve.

Backstrap Medallions in a Cabernet-Mushroom Reduction

Ingredients:

- Venison backstrap, trimmed of all fat and silver skin, then cut crosswise into eight ¾" medallions
- 1 cup beef broth
- 1 cup cabernet sauvignon
- 2 Tbsp olive oil
- 4 Tbsp butter, divided
- 2 Tbsp dry rub or grill seasoning
- 1 shallot, diced finely
- 2 garlic cloves, diced finely
- 1 cup cremini mushrooms, sliced
- Kosher salt and coarsely ground black pepper, to taste

Preparation:

1. Combine the broth and wine in a small sauce pan over medium-high heat. Bring to a low boil, then reduce the heat to medium low and simmer until the liquid is reduced by half.
2. Heat the oil and 2 Tbsp of the butter in a large, heavy-bottomed sauté pan until it the butter begins to sizzle. Cook the medallions for 3 minutes on each side, then remove them to plate and cover loosely with foil.
3. Reduce the heat to medium and sauté the shallots and mushrooms until they soften, then add the garlic. Add the wine/broth mixture and simmer until the sauce thickens.
4. Stir in the remaining butter and simmer until it is thoroughly melted and integrated into the sauce. Taste and add salt and pepper as needed.
5. Pour the sauce into a gravy boat and serve immediately with the medallions.

Garlic-Roasted Baby Carrots & Okra

Ingredients:

- 6 or 7 baby carrots, washed & rinsed, with stalks removed, then sliced lengthwise
- 2 cups okra, washed & rinsed, sliced cross-wise
- ¼ cup olive oil
- 1 Tbsp granulated garlic
- ½ Tbsp coarsely ground black pepper
- ½ tsp Kosher salt

Preparation:

1. Preheat the oven to 400° F.
2. Pour the olive oil in a medium non-reactive mixing bowl and toss the carrots and okra in the oil until well covered. Sprinkle the garlic, pepper and salt over the mixture, making sure that each piece is spiced.
3. Place the carrots and okra on a cookie sheet and place in the oven for 15 to 18 minutes, taking care to avoid burning or overcooking.
4. Transfer to a serving bowl and serve immediately.

Suggested Accompaniment:

- **Syrah:** Stolpman Estate (Santa Ynez, California)
- **Carmenere:** Tierra Alta Gran Reserve (Chile)

Broiled Baby Carrots & Okra   Arugula w/Sliced Plums, Walnuts & Raspberry Balsamic Vinegar
Venison Backstrap Medallions   Cabernet-Mushroom Reduction

Gator Bait!

"There are a lot of Bream in our community pond," our friend Joanne said when I mentioned having gone bream fishing with my friend David and his two grandsons. "The pond is only for residents of our development, but you can fish it as my guest if you want to."

Of course I wanted to! I still have fond memories of fishing for rainbow trout in small ponds around western Washington State, rowing a small inflatable rubber raft, trolling various wet flies behind me. Unfortunately, I no longer had a raft, but Joanne volunteered the use of her fiberglass kayak.

"Have you ever used a kayak before?" she asked.

"Sure – but it has been a while!" I replied.

"I don't know how you're going to be able to paddle and fish at the same time, but you're welcome to use it any time you want," she said, looking more than a little skeptical.

A couple of days later, I decided to venture out. Joanne was at work, but the kayak wasn't locked up, and she had left a small wagon on which I could balance the boat to transport it to the pond's edge, so I loaded my gear into the kayak, pulled it onto the wagon, and set off.

A short time later, as I slid the small but heavy boat down the bank into the water, I noticed an eight- or nine-foot alligator watching me intently from twenty yards away as it floated motionlessly on the glassy water. I didn't think much of it, figuring that it was highly unlikely that the gator would come after me, but I was a little concerned that its presence might bother the fish.

I climbed into the boat clumsily but safely, and paddled slowly away from the bank, and was relieved when the 'gator decided not to follow me! A few minutes later, I cast my 8-foot fly rod and made my way down the bank as the line sank below the surface.

The afternoon was warm and calm, with just enough of a breeze to keep me cool, but I hadn't had so much as a nibble after an hour, so I changed flies to a red and gray "Woolie Bugger" that imitated a caddis fly larva. Although I highly doubted that there are any caddis flies in southeastern Georgia, it seemed to do the trick: a few minutes after I tied it on, the rod tip jerked spasmodically – and hard.

I should have practiced what I needed to do when I got a bite, because what I needed to do wasn't exactly easy: I had to swing the boat around 180° to face the fleeing fish, lay the oar across my lap, pick up the rod without knocking the oar into the water, play the fish to the boat, then net or unhook it – all while keeping my balance!

Fortunately, by taking each step slowly, I managed to get turned around and play the fish to the boat without a mishap. It fought hard, and I quickly decided that it wasn't a bream. Sure enough, it wasn't a bream: it was an alligator gar of about twenty-five inches! I had no idea that there were any alligator gar in the area, let alone this little pond, until I remembered that there was a canal leading from the pond to the nearby Ogeechee River – in  which I had heard that gar could be found. I guess that this one had made its way up the canal to the pond and decided to stay.

Getting the fish to the boat was easy enough, but I didn't have a clue how to extract the hook from its long snout lined with lots of sharp teeth! I didn't have a hemostat, so I grabbed the fish tightly behind the head and carefully twisted and pulled the fly until it came loose from the jaw. None the worse for wear, the fish sped toward the bottom of the pond where it would probably sulk for a while!

I flipped the fly back into the water before picking up the oar and continuing down the shoreline. Glancing over my shoulder from time to time, I noticed that a dead tree had fallen into the water, jutting out nearly thirty feet from the bank. That had to be perfect habitat for bream, I thought.

Paddling slowly along the shore, then alongside the tree, I could see little fish scurry from the outer limbs toward the trunk. There HAD to be some adults here, too! The fly, trailing behind me, was about two or three feet below the surface about fifteen feet behind the boat, and I knew that when a fish struck, it would head directly down and toward the trunk, doing its best to tangle in the tree branches and break the line.

As I swung the boat around the outside end of the branches, a strong jerk on the rod tip signaled that a fish had grabbed the fly. I carefully turned the boat around, lifted the rod, and laid the oar across the cockpit. Fortunately, the fish had decided to head for deep water away from the tree, so I was able to play him without having to deal with the branches. He was a real fighter, peeling line from the reel on several short runs. My leader was only two-pound test, so it made more sense to let him run and tire himself out than to try to drag him in.

Bringing the fish alongside the boat, I was in for another surprise: he wasn't a bream; he was a crappie – and was much darker than any other crappie I'd ever seen. As I grasped his lip and lifted him into the boat, I realized that he was a black crappie, and weighed almost two pounds!

I slipped the hook from his jaw and dropped him into a small cooler, knowing that he'd be great eating. As I tossed the fly over the side of the kayak and began to turn the boat around to continue down the bank, however, I moved too quickly and felt the boat begin to roll. I tried to lean back the other way to steady it, but it didn't work, and within a few short seconds, I found myself enjoying the cool water! Fortunately, it was only about four feet deep, but as I turned to grab the kayak and the oar, I noticed that the alligator was floating on the surface watching my graceless water ballet from about thirty feet away!

I didn't really think that the gator would come after me, but I also didn't want to wait around to find out, so I pulled the boat as quickly as I could toward the shore. The gator hovered for several  minutes, unmoving, as I gathered the gear that had spilled out of the boat's cockpit. As it happened, the only loss or damage was my ego!

Now soaking wet, but otherwise none the worse for wear, I put everything back in order and climbed back into the kayak. I had only covered about half of the pond and only had one fish in the cooler, so I flipped the fly behind the boat and resumed course as if nothing had happened.

Continuing down the shoreline, I found several weed beds and stumps that harbored fish, and soon had half a dozen decent-sized bream to go with the crappie. My clothes were nearly dry, and I had built up a terrific thirst, so I decided to call it a day. Magically, after not having appeared since my little 'mishap,' the gator glided into view to watch my departure. Although only a short time earlier I had almost been gator bait, I knew that it's always better to eat than be eaten!

Iceberg Lettuce Wedges w/Creamy Blue Cheese Dressing

Ingredients:

- 4 slices of thick-cut bacon
- 1 cup low-fat mayonnaise
- ½ cup blue cheese, divided
- ½ cup non-fat half & half
- 3 Tbsp low- or non-fat sour cream
- 1 Tbsp lemon juice
- ½ tsp Worchester sauce
- ¼ tsp Kosher salt
- ½ tsp coarsely ground black pepper
- 1 head fresh iceberg lettuce, chilled and sliced vertically into 8 wedges

Preparation:

1. Fry the bacon until crisp; remove to a paper towel-covered plate to drain.
2. In a medium non-reactive mixing bowl, combine the mayonnaise, ¼ cup of the blue cheese, the half and half, the sour cream, the lemon juice, the Worcestershire sauce, and the salt. Whisk until smooth.
3. Gently stir in the remaining ¼ cup blue cheese and season with pepper to taste.
4. Place each wedge on a salad plate and spoon the dressing over the lettuce.
5. Crumble the bacon over the top of the dressing and serve.

Blackened Black Crappie Fillets

Ingredients:

- 8 Black Crappies, cleaned and scaled, then filleted – with skin left on
- 3 Tbsp olive oil
- 2 Tbsp butter
- 1½ - 2 tsp blackened seasoning

Preparation:

1. Heat the oil and butter over medium-high heat in a large, heavy-bottomed sauté pan.
2. Pour the blackened seasoning in a shallow bowl and dredge each fillet in the seasoning. Place each fillet skin side up in the pan, and sauté for 4 to 5 minutes. Flip each fillet and continue cooking for another 3 to 4 minutes, or until the flesh is opaque.
3. Remove the fillets to a serving platter and serve.

Sweet Potato Oven Fries

Ingredients:

- 3 medium or 2 large sweet potatoes, washed, peeled and sliced into fries
- 2 Tbsp olive oil
- 1 tsp mild chili powder
- ½ tsp black pepper
- ½ tsp Kosher salt
- Vegetable cooking spray

Preparation:

1. Preheat the oven to 425°F.
2. In a large mixing bowl, coat the potatoes in the olive oil, then sprinkle with the chili powser, salt and pepper to coat evenly.
3. Spread the potatoes on a cookie sheet and bake for20 minutes. Turn the potatoes over and bake for another 10 minutes.
4. Remove to a paper napkin-lined bowl or basket and serve.

Suggested Accompaniment:

- **Pinot Gris:** Elk Cove (Oregon)
- **Beer:** Anchor Steam India Pale Ale (San Francisco, California)

Blackened Black Crappie Fillet

Fish For Dinner – Creekside!

One of the things I enjoy about living near the coast is having access to lots of tidal creeks and their diversity of wildlife. One – Tivoli Creek – is less than five miles from my front door and has a public-access dock from which residents can fish for spot-tail bass, speckled trout, whiting and croakers, throw cast nets for shrimp, bird watch, and catch blue crabs.

An added benefit of having such great public access and facilities is that you meet a lot of friendly and interesting people: retirees, military personnel and their families taking a break from their duties on nearby Fort Stewart, and kayakers launching from the dock for a quick paddle up or down the creek, to name a few.

Mother Nature was, indeed, smiling late one afternoon in early October as I made the short drive to the Creek: It was beautifully clear, with mild temperatures and a light breeze across the marsh. The tide was about half-way out when I arrived, and the wet, muddy edges of the creek glistened as they sloped away from the marsh grasses. Gulls soared above, and great white herons and snowy egrets stalked along the water's edge up and down the creek.

Baiting my crab traps with raw chicken back pieces, I lowered them into the slowly ebbing water below the dock and sat back to enjoy the scenery.

Within a few minutes after I lowered the last trap to the creek bottom, Willie, an amiable retired mill worker I had met earlier that year, ambled down the ramp. We shook hands and asked how the other was doing, then Willie went about setting his traps.

Typically, I leave my traps in the water for about ten minutes before checking them. Many people opt for longer 'sets,' but I haven't seen any difference between their results and mine, and I'm too antsy to let them sit any longer! Today was no exception, and ten minutes later I quickly hauled the first trap to the surface. As it rose out of the murky flow, I saw two keeper-sized crabs scrambling to escape.

"You already caught some?" Willie asked, incredulous. "I've barely got my traps in the water!"

"Yep. I've found that if there are crabs in the area, they'll come right to the bait. If there aren't any crabs around, a longer wait may or may not work," I replied.

I lifted the trap over the dock railing and set it in the center of the wooden dock, then quickly put my foot on the crabs (one at a time, of course!) firmly enough to pin them to the dock, grabbed each claw from behind to keep them from pinching me, then untangled each beast from the wire mesh and quickly deposited it into a deep plastic bucket. Repeating the process with each trap, I ended up with three keepers. As each trap was cleared, I lowered it back into the water to begin another set.

"You must have some kind of super scent on your bait!" Willie exclaimed. "I've never caught three crabs that soon!"

"Nah," I responded. "I think we just caught the tide right, and I'm guessing that they haven't had much pressure for a few days."

The beautiful afternoon rolled slowly toward sunset, and Willie and I had managed to each catch seven or eight crabs – a couple of which were very large for the creek – as we talked about the benefits and drawbacks of retirement and our dysfunctional government. The outgoing tide was nearly at its low point, and the breeze across the marsh was just enough to keep the bugs away. In other words, perfect!

The 'bite' began to taper off, and we were talking about packing it it when we were both befuddled at a commotion coming towards us from downstream. Gulls were swarming above roiling water, screeching and chattering loudly. As we both focused on the calamity, we were soon able to make out several dorsal fins, announced by sprays of mist, of a pod of dolphins racing up the creek.

"They're herding bait fish!" I blurted out. "Watch this!" Seconds later, two or three dolphins at the head of the pod plowed their way up the sloping mud bank, snapping to catch several six- to eight-inch mullets that they had chased ashore. As the first dolphins caught their prey, they flopped themselves back down the bank as others roared up behind them.

In less than a minute, the feeding frenzy was over, and the dolphins were re-grouping in the center of the creek.

"That was amazing!" Willie exclaimed. "Have you ever seen anything like that?"

"I've seen it on one of those National Geographic nature shows, but not in person! This is wild!" I responded. "I'm sure glad I was able to get a picture!"

The spectacle wasn't over, though, as the pod continued their path up-current toward the dock. Their hunting strategy quickly became apparent, as three or four pod members broke away from the pack and cruised out ahead of the main group. They crisscrossed back and forth from bank to bank, clearly searching for more bait fish, and had gone no more than a hundred yards or so before one of the hunters slapped the surface of the water with its tail, apparently signaling the rest that prey had been located.

The rest of the pod quickly shifted into high gear, racing toward the advance scouts, and chased another school of mullets up onto the slick, muddy bank. The hapless fish flopped and wriggled as the marauders thrashed and snapped their jaws, capturing their silvery prey, before sliding back into the roiling water, making way for their pod-mates to do the same.

Having flopped their way back down the slick mud bank, the dolphins soon re-grouped and continued their way up the creek – past the dock and under the bridge. Willie and I both knew that about a mile upstream the water would become too shallow for them to swim further, but by the time they reached that point, the tide would turn and they'd make their way back down the estuary to St. Catherine's Sound.

"I've lived here my whole life and thought I'd seen 'bout everythin', but I sure never saw nothin' like that!" Willie said, shaking his head in disbelief.

"I'll send you a copy of this picture if you'd like," I replied.

"I'm gonna need a picture, else no one's ever gonna believe me!" he said, laughing.

We chatted about the upcoming winter, wondering whether it would be as dry as the past summer had been, and about how much longer we'd be able to catch crabs as we raised our traps for the last time that day and lugged them to our cars.

As I turned for one last look over the creek and out across the marsh beyond it, I couldn't help but appreciate the beauty and serenity, even knowing that dramas of life and death were happening as far as I could see. The egrets and herons stealthily ambushing minnows and fiddler crabs along the shoreline, marsh hens cackling to each other from their grassy hide-aways, and the dolphins – quiet but deadly in their quest for a meal – were all part of the spectrum of unique and unusual sights and sounds on this beautiful afternoon as they had fish for dinner – creekside!

Cajun-Style Caesar Salad

Ingredients:

- Vegetable cooking spray
- ½ loaf thick-sliced French bread, cut into ¾" cubes
- 2 Tbsp butter
- 2 Tbsp Cajun seasoning
- 4 cups romaine lettuce leaves, washed, rinsed, patted dry and chopped
- ½ cup Caesar salad dressing
- ½ cup grated fresh parmesan cheese, divided
- 4 anchovy filets, chopped (optional)

Preparation:

1. Preheat the oven to 400° F. Lightly coat a cookie sheet with the vegetable spray.
2. Melt the butter in a large mixing bowl; toss the bread cubes gently to coat evenly, then sprinkle on the Cajun seasoning, continuing to toss gently. Spread the cubes evenly on the cookie sheet and bake for 12 - 15 minutes or until crispy, but be careful to avoid burning.
3. In a large salad bowl, toss the lettuce leaves and dressing to coat evenly. Add the toasted bread cubes and toss gently. Sprinkle with ¼ cup of the parmesan cheese, reserving the rest for the table. Divide onto 4 salad plates, placing an anchovy filet on the top of each salad, if desired.

She Crab Soup

Ingredients:

- 3 Tbsp extra virgin olive oil
- ½ cup chopped celery
- ¼ cup chopped carrots
- ¼ cup chopped onion
- ¼ pound butter or margarine
- ¾ cup flour
- 1 cup fat-free half & half or fat-free sour cream
- 4 cups milk
- 2 cups chicken or seafood soup base
- ¼ pound crab roe (if available)
- 1 pound lump or blue crab meat
- ¼ cup sherry, plus ¼ tsp per serving bowl, divided
- ½ tsp Tabasco Sauce
- 1 Tbsp Worcestershire Sauce
- 4 tsp fat-free sour cream, divided
- 1 tsp sherry, divided

Preparation:

1. Heat the olive oil in a 4 quart stock pot over medium high heat. Add the celery, carrots and onion; saute until softened.
2. Add the butter or margarine and stir occasionally until melted.
3. Stir in the flour to make a roux, then add the half-& half or sour cream and milk and slowly bring it to a boil.
4. Add the soup base, crab roe and meat, celery, carrots, onion, sherry, Tabasco and Worcestershire sauces and reduce the heat to medium low.
5. Simmer for 20 minutes, garnish each bowl with a dollop of sour cream and ¼ tsp of sherry.

Tuscan Artisan Bread

Ingredients:

- 1½ Tbsp dry yeast
- 1½ Tbsp coarse grey sea salt
- 3 cups warm water
- 6½ cups unbleached, all-purpose flour, plus more for dusting
- 1 Tbsp cornmeal

Preparation:

1. In a large bowl, mix the yeast and salt into the 3 cups of warm water. Once the water begins to foam, add the flour and stir to combine completely.

2. Let the dough rise, covered in a warm place for at least two hours, until it rises and collapses – up to 5 hours. The dough may be baked at this point, or refrigerated for later use.

3. Cover the dough, but make sure it is not airtight so that gases can escape – and place it in the refrigerator until you are ready to use it.

4. Dust a flat, clean surface with flour and use a serrated knife to cut off a grapefruit-sized piece of dough. Turning the dough in your hands, stretch the surface of the dough and tuck in under so that the surface is smooth and the bottom is bunched.

5. Sprinkle the flat surface with cornmeal and roll the dough in it. Allow the dough to rest in a warm place for 40 minutes – longer if you make a larger loaf.

6. Twenty minutes before baking, preheat the oven to 450°F with a baking stone or overturned baking sheet inside on the middle rack and a shallow metal pan on the top rack. Dust the top of the dough with a small fistful of flour, slash it in a cross, a tic-tac-toe, or a fan), and place it on the baking stone. Pour one to two cups of tap water into the metal pan on the top rack and quickly shut the oven door to trap steam inside. Bake for 30 minutes, or until the crust is well browned and the bread sounds hollow when you rap it on the bottom with your knuckles.

Suggested Accompaniment:

- **Fume Blanc:** Ste. Jean (Sonoma Valley, California)
- **Chardonney:** 14 Hands (Columbia Valley, Washington)

She-Crab Soup

Big Ass Boar!

"This has GOT to be the biggest 'tree' stand I've ever seen!" I said, quietly, as I climbed the wooden ladder toward the platform high above.

"That's why they named it the "Big Ass Stand!" my friend David replied with a big grin on his face.

It was early January, but with the weather still pleasant, David had suggested that we go to our hunting lease property near Hinesville, Georgia for a late-season deer hunt. Facing a little over a forty-minute drive, we decided to leave at 1:30 p.m., to be in the stand by 2:30 p.m. The afternoon was sunny and crisp as the temperature hovered around forty degrees.

True to its name, the Big Ass Stand consisted of a solid fifteen-foot square platform with three-foot sides and two-by-four railings hovering thirty feet off the ground, anchored on each side to telephone poles! The platform comfortably fit four folding chairs, and from its location and height, it provided a clear view of nearly a mile straight ahead and to our left down a power line.

As we settled in, we noticed that someone had written yardages to key landmarks – 120 yards to a wooden stake on the far corner of the nearest food plot and 175 yards to a game trail leaving the power line on the other side, plus various other points in each direction. In all, there were three good-sized food plots in clear view – the farthest being several hundred yards straight ahead. The absence of a yardage to that plot later proved to be very unfortunate!

It was nearly 3:00 by the time we got settled in, but that still left a little over an hour and a half until dark. There was a high school between us and the main highway into Hinesville, and they were apparently having a soccer game because yells from a small crowd and shrill blasts from a referee's whistle cut the air.

"I hope that noise doesn't bother the game!" I whispered to David,

"Nah, it won't bother 'em. They hear it every day, so they're used to it!" he replied.

A short time later, I spotted a small flock of turkeys as they emerged from the woods into the power line. I slowly tapped David on the shoulder and pointed at them, whispering "Can you see the turkeys? I think they might head our way." It took David a minute to spot them, and by the time he was sure that the birds were turkeys rather than crows, they were coming towards us in a scraggly single file.

The birds were nearly a half mile away when we first saw them. They stopped to scratch the ground, chase each other in a frantic game of tag, and crane their necks looking for trouble, so it took them nearly forty-five minutes to make their way to our stand.

By the time they strolled past, the light had started to fade. "They're headed down to that patch of trees to roost," David said. I nodded in reply, turning my head to the food plot on our left hoping that a deer had snuck out to feed while we were fixated on the turkeys. No such luck!

There was less than fifteen minutes of shooting light left when I looked toward the food plot in the distance. Spotting movement but not being able to identify it, I thought my eyes were playing tricks on me.

"What is that?" I whispered to David, pointing. We both raised our binoculars but had to wait several seconds for the apparition to move out from behind a small bush.

"That's a hog," David calmly replied. "And it looks to be a pretty decent sized one. "You should shoot it!"

I liked that idea, and slowly brought my .243 caliber rifle to my shoulder and anchored it on the two-by-four railing. "How far do you think it is?" I asked David. Even through my 3 X 9 scope, the critter still looked a long way off. "I'd say 280 to 290 yards," David replied, studying the hog in his binoculars. We couldn't be sure, both of us having left our range finders at home!

I placed the scope's crosshairs about two inches below the back line directly above his shoulder and squeezed the trigger slowly. The gun roared as flame spat from the barrel. As quickly as I could, I brought the scope back on the hog, hoping to see it lying in a heap. The black beast continued to feed, clearly unfazed, in the middle of the food plot.

"Try 325," David said as I ejected the first shell and chambered another. Exhaling completely, I squeezed the trigger and the gun roared again. Again, the hog fed on, oblivious to my attempts to murder it!

"You try," I said, turning to David. "You're a much better shot, and maybe we're just not guessing the yardage correctly. Your scope has yardage beads so that should help. Besides, it'll be dark in two minutes, and I'm clearly not getting the job done!"

"OK," David said. "I'd much rather you kill it, but I can't disagree with you!"

Taking my place at the railing, he brought his scope into focus on the hog as it grazed. A moment later, his rifle spat flame into the near-darkness, and, as I watched through my binoculars, the hog dropped like a sack of potatoes.

"You got it!" I nearly shouted.

"Yeah, but you didn't have a fair chance," he replied.

"What do you mean?" I asked.

"When I fit one of the yardage beads on the hog before I shot, it was over 400 yards!"

"400 yards!?" I exclaimed, agape.

"At least. I think it was a little more, but not enough to matter," he replied.

By the time we gathered our gear, we had to use our flashlights to climb down from the stand. We figured that it wouldn't be a big deal retrieving the hog, since it was just a short way (by truck) up the power line. Boy, were we wrong!

As David got the truck, I walked up the power line toward the hog. About 100 yards from the stand, however, I encountered water beneath the thick grass, and it quickly deepened. We certainly hadn't planned to wade to get the hog!.

We quickly decided to drive around the property to the power line about a mile above the stand. After a twenty minute drive, we left the truck in pitch dark.

About 100 yards from the truck, we again encountered water. If there was any good news, the road sloped downward toward the food plot and the water wouldn't get as deep as on the stand side. After a short discussion (and more than a little cussing!), we decided not to leave the hog unattended overnight. We weren't concerned about the meat spoiling, but there were coyotes and other carnivores that might get to it, so we'd just have to deal with the discomfort.

Sloshing through the marshy weeds, we eventually reached the hog and determined that it was a boar: about 300 pounds of boar! It wasn't 'rutted up,' though, and I looked forward to getting it home to the freezer.

There was no way we were going to be able to drag a beast this size a mile uphill to the truck, even if most of it was through shin-deep water. So, we field dressed it, dragged it to a nearby oak tree and hoisted it as high as we could off the ground. Even if coyotes found it, they probably wouldn't mess with it because of our scent.

The next morning, we loaded David's four-wheeler into the bed of his truck and set out to retrieve our trophy. I brought hip waders, and the four-wheeler rode high enough to keep David out of the water, and we soon arrived at the oak tree.

"It looks a lot bigger in the daylight!" I exclaimed as we lowered it onto the back of the four-wheeler.

"Of course it is! It's a Big Ass Boar!" David chuckled.

Blue Crab Ravioli w/Lemon-Dill Sauce

Pasta Ingredients:

- 2 cups all-purpose flour, plus additional for dusting
- 2 eggs at room temperature
- ½ tsp Kosher salt
- 4 to 6 Tbsp cold water

Preparation:

1. Pour the flour into a large mixing bowl in a mound, and make a crater in the center. Add the egg and salt and beat the eggs lightly, then stir in 2 Tbsp of the water with a large wooden spoon. Using a circular motion, draw in flour from the sides of the crater a little at a time. Add 1 Tbsp of water and continue to stir until all of the flour is evenly moistened. If necessary, stir in more water, a little at a time. When the dough becomes too thick to stir, use your hands to finish mixing.
2. Pat the dough into a ball and knead it a few times to make sure that the flour absorbs all of the water.
3. Prepare a flat, clean work surface and due with flour.
4. Remove the dough ball to the work surface and knead it again a couple of times, flatten it, then fold the farthest edge toward you. With the heel of your hand, press and push the dough away from you until the fold is sealed completely. Rotate the dough ¼ turn and repeat the folding-sealing process. Continue this same step for about 10 minutes, then cover the dough and let it rest for about 20 minutes.
5. Divide the dough in half and roll it flat, rotating and flipping it occasionally, until it is about 10" × 12". Repeat with the other half of the dough

Sauce Ingredients:

- 1 egg, beaten
- 1 cup sugar
- juice of 2 lemons, about 4 to 6 Tbsp
- grated lemon zest of 1 lemon
- 1 tablespoon butter
- 2 Tbsp fresh dill, chopped

Preparation:

1. In a small saucepan over low heat, combine the egg, sugar, lemon juice and lemon zest and cook, stirring constantly until the mixture thickens. Add the butter and dill and stir until the butter is completely melted and incorporated.
2. Keep warm until the raviolis are ready to serve, then spoon over the raviolis.

Ravioli Ingredients:

- 1 Tbsp butter
- ¼ cup minced sweet onion
- ¼ cup minced celery
- 1 cup fresh blue crab meat, carefully picked and rinsed
- 1 tsp Dijon mustard
- 2 Tbsp half n half
- 1 egg, lightly beaten
- 2 Tbsp lemon juice
- 2 Tbsp fresh basil, chopped finely
- ¼ cup plain bread crumbs
- Kosher salt, to taste
- Two 8" × 10" sheets of fresh pasta dough*
- 1 egg, lightly beaten
- 2 Qts fresh water
- ½ tsp olive oil (optional)
- Dash Kosher salt (optional)

Preparation:

1. In a small sauté pan over medium heat, melt the butter until it foams. Add the onion and celery, then reduce the temperature to low after two minutes. Cook, stirring often, for about 15 minutes. Remove from the heat.
2. In a medium mixing bowl, combine the crab meat, mustard, half n half, egg, lemon juice, basil, salt and bread crumbs. Toss to mix well, then add the onion-celery mixture. Toss again to incorporate.
3. Cut each sheet of the pasta dough into 2" × 2" squares. One at a time, brush a square with egg, spoon on about 1 tsp of the crab mixture, cover with another square and seal the edges by pressing down on the pasta with the tines of a fork. Repeat until all squares have been used or the crab mixture is gone.
4. Bring the water – with the olive oil and salt, if desired – to a boil. Add the raviolis in batches of 5 or 6 and cook until they rise to the surface, then cook for an additional 1 minute. Remove and drain. Repeat until all 20 raviolis are cooked and drained.
5. Divide the raviolis into shallow serving bowls or plates, spoon the sauce over the top and serve immediately.

Honey-Gingered Baby Carrots

Ingredients:

- 2 Tbsp honey
- ½ Tbsp fresh ginger, grated
- 1 Tbsp white balsamic vinegar
- 2 cups baby carrots, washed & peeled, with tops removed
- 1 Tbsp fresh parsley, chopped

Preparation:

1. Whisk the honey, ginger and vinegar together in a small mixing bowl.
2. Steam the carrots until tender. Remove to a serving bowl.
3. Pour the honey mixture over the carrots, tossing gently.
4. Sprinkle the chopped parsley over the carrots and serve immediately.

Wild Boar Chops in an Onion-Pepper-Pear Ragout

Ingredients:

- Eight bone-in wild boar rib chops
- ⅓ cup all-purpose flour
- 2 medium yellow onions, peeled and sliced thinly from top to bottom
- ½ green, ½ yellow and ½ orange bell pepper, sliced thinly
- 1 ripe Bosch pear, quartered lengthwise, then chopped into ½" cubes
- 2 Tbsp olive oil
- 1 Tbsp butter
- ¼ cup Marsala wine
- ½ cup chicken soup base (dissolved) or stock

Preparation:

1. Heat the oil and butter to sizzling over medium-high heat in a heavy-bottomed saute pan.
1. Dredge the chops in the flour, shaking off any excess.
2. Reduce the heat to medium, then saute the chops for 4-5 minutes per side. Remove the chops to a platter and cover loosely with foil.
3. Add the onions to the pan and sauté until they become tender. Add the peppers and sauté, stirring, until the peppers become tender. Add the wine and the broth; cook, stirring, until reduced by ½. Add the pear cubes and gently stir them into the ragout.
4. Return the chops to the pan to heat, then serve; the ragout can be spooned over the top or served separately.

Suggested Accompaniment:

- **Pinot Noir:** Lucky Star (California)
- **Cabernet Sauvignon:** Baron V (Columbia Valley, Washington)

Wild Boar Chops

Shrimps and 'Shrooms

I will be the first person to admit that my skills at throwing a shrimp net are mediocre at best. Regardless, I do manage to catch a few of the critters from time to time, and my lack of skill doesn't keep me home when the shrimp are running: after all, I can almost always catch enough blue crabs to fill the cooler even if I don't catch any shrimp!

So, when my friend David called one morning after three days of gray skies and intermittent rain to tell me that his son had caught 'a mess' of shrimp that morning, I quickly agreed to meet him at the dock on Tivoli Creek. The sky had cleared, and a gentle breeze wafted out of the northwest. I quickly checked the tide chart to confirm that it would be outgoing for another 3 to 4 hours.

Before loading the crab traps and bait, and the shrimp net into my car, I decided to check to see if the shiitake mushrooms my wife and I grow in our back yard had begun their fall growth. I attached a spray nozzle to the garden hose and dragged it behind me to the mushroom 'garden.' Five three-foot-long oak logs were leaned vertically against PVC center posts, and each log had been drilled with about forth ⅜" holes into which we had stuffed sawdust mixed with mushroom spores before sealing each hole with paraffin wax. Once the crop was 'planted,' we sprayed the logs at least three times a week – if the rain didn't do it for us.

Sure enough, when I approached the 'garden,' I saw that several small 'shrooms' had popped out of some holes on several logs, and a handful were already almost large enough to harvest, even though there hadn't been any sign of growth only four days earlier. This strain of 'shroom was noted for its quick growth and, if left alone, its large size. It wasn't unusual, in fact, for them to reach

5 to 6 inches diameter and 1 to 1½ inches thick! Seeing a few large enough to harvest, though, set my mouth watering as I imagined enjoying them with fresh shrimp and crabs. Mmmm Mmmm good!

David was already at the creek waiting for me; he doesn't crab or shrimp himself but is almost always ready to hang out with me, have a cigar (or two!) and swap stories. The tide had just started to ebb, which usually meant that the shrimp would be coming out of the marsh grass soon.

Chatting with David about the upcoming deer season, I set the crab traps with chicken backs and a couple of minnows each, then headed down the ramp to the floating dock segment with the shrimp net.

"Thank you!" David said, smiling.

"For what?" I answered.

"For bringing that shrimp net. I haven't had a good laugh in a while!" he chuckled.

I unrolled the net from its attached rope, slipped the loop at the end of the rope onto my wrist, and gathered the net to make a cast. I took one of the lead weights lining the bottom edge of the net between my teeth and a couple of others gathered in my left hand. Turning slowly to the right, then twirling to the left, I released the net as it fanned out before hitting the surface of the creek.

"That wasn't too bad!" David said from the railing above me.

"Thank You!" I responded. "Maybe I'll figure this out yet!"

The weights around the circumference of the net quickly pulled it to the bottom. The circle would then close as I hoisted it back toward me, trapping any shrimp or small fish in the net.

As I lifted the net onto the dock, I saw two decent-sized shrimp wriggling in the net. Obviously, more would have been great, but it was a good start. I carefully unfolded the net and extracted the shrimp, finding a couple of smaller victims in the process. I dropped the two larger critters in a bucket with a couple inches of creek water.

"Thirty more casts like that and you'll have enough for dinner!" David jibed.

"Yeah, well, I plan to catch a few crabs, too!" I replied as I gathered the net for another cast.

About half of the next seven or eight casts were decent, and another six shrimp joined the first two in the bucket before I set the net on the dock and climbed the ramp to check the crab traps. Three of the four traps held 'keeper-sized' blue crabs with shell spans of 5 inches or more.

"Well, sir, a couple more crabs and another dozen shrimp and I'll have a pretty good meal!" I said to David as I lit a cigar.

"Are you going to eat them together?" he asked.

"Yeah, I think I'll try a new recipe tonight – shrimp and grits with corn and shallots.

"What the heck is a shallot?!" he replied. David's usual shrimp dinner involves breading and cocktail sauce, so adding something to the grits wasn't something he would do!

"It's easy. I make a batch of grits, then add fresh corn cut off the cob, with shallots – small, sweet onions – then add cooked shrimp," I explained.

"I might have to try that – it sounds pretty good!" David said thoughtfully.

A few minutes later, I resumed casting for shrimp, but on the third cast, it caught on something on the creek bottom. I tugged on the rope a couple of times but didn't want to pull so hard that I ripped the net.

"Come up here" David said from the railing above me. "Pulling from a different angle might do the trick."

Keeping tension on the rope – to keep more of the net from tangling on whatever had snagged it – I climbed the ramp to where David stood, then pulled a little harder from the opposite direction. It began to move, but the net was clearly still caught on something. I pulled slowly and gently, and the net began to move toward the surface. As the top of the net became visible near the water's surface, I moved back down the ramp to the lower dock, then lifted the net carefully onto the wooden deck, revealing a nearly new crab trap that had been snagged by the net.

"It looks as though someone's crab trap got caught on the oysters," I said, referring to a small oyster bed we had noticed previously at low tide.

"It looks new, too," David said. Do you have any extra rope?" referring to the braided nylon rope used to attach the crab traps.

A quick run to the car and a little tying and re-baiting later, I lowered the new trap over the dock railing and returned to the lower deck for a couple more casts. And, after adding another six shrimp to the bucket, I agreed with David's suggestion that I should quit while I was ahead. I folded up the cast net and returned it to its carrying container and climbed back up the ramp to talk with David about hunting the following week.

As we finished our cigars and I began to pack up for the day, the wind picked up out of the southwest and a thundercloud appeared on the horizon.

"Looks like our timing is good!" David commented as the first raindrops hit the wooden deck.

"Yeah, it is! I was done anyhow, but a downpour sure ends all doubt!" I said as the last crab trap cleared the railing.

In all, we had about 15 shrimp and eight crabs – a couple of which were well over 6 inches – and I was looking forward to shrimp and grits for dinner!

Mixed Greens w/Pickled Mushrooms

Pickled Mushroom Ingredients:

- 1½ cups cremini mushrooms, sliced
- ¾ cup low sodium soy sauce
- ½ cup rice vinegar
- ½ cup sugar
- 2 Tbsp sweet rice wine
- 1 Tbsp sesame oil
- 1" piece of fresh ginger, peeled and chopped
- 2 cloves fresh garlic, minced
- ¼ tsp crushed red pepper (optional)
- sesame seeds
- ½ cup cold water
- 1 green onion, chopped finely

Salad Ingredients:

- 2 cups mixed baby greens
- ¼ cup peeled and washed carrots, shredded
- 1 green onion, sliced cross-wise
- ½ cup pickled Shi'itake mushrooms
- 1 Tbsp olive oil
- 1 Tbsp balsamic vinegar

Preparation:

1. Combine the all of the ingredients except the green onion, in a medium saucepan. Add just enough water to cover, then bring the mixture to a boil. Reduce the heat and simmer about 20 to 30 minutes until mushrooms are very dark and soft. Adjust the vinegar and soy sauce as needed. They should be a little sweet/sour and a little salty.

2. Remove from heat to cool and stir in the green onion. When cool, refrigerate in a non-reactive, tightly sealed container. The mixture will keep for 2 to 3 weeks in the refrigerator.

Preparation:

1. Combine the greens, carrots and onion in a medium salad bowl. Toss to mix. Top with the mushrooms.

2. In a small bowl or cruet, combine the oil and vinegar and mix thoroughly.

3. Sprinkle the oil and vinegar over the salad and serve immediately.

Shrimp & Grits w/Shallots, Corn and Scallions

For the Grits:

- 2½ cups chicken stock
- 2 Tbsp butter
- ½ cup Stone-Ground grits
- 2 cups low- or fat-free sour cream
- Kosher salt and coarsely ground black pepper, to taste
- ½ tsp red pepper flakes (optional)

Preparation:

1. Bring the stock and butter to a boil in a heavy-bottomed medium sauce pan. Stir in the grits and return the liquid to a boil.
2. Reduce the heat to a simmer and cook the grits for another 15 minutes, stirring constantly, until the grits have absorbed most of the stock. Add the sour cream ½ cup at a time, stirring for about 10 minutes to integrate each portion before adding the next. Add the salt and pepper to taste.
3. Remove to a large bowl and cover.

For the Shrimp:

- 2 Tbsp extra virgin olive oil, divided
- ½ cup shallots, chopped
- 1 cup fresh or frozen corn
- ¼ cup red bell pepper, diced
- ½ tsp dried thyme
- 1 lb medium shrimp, peeled and deveined
- Kosher salt & coarsely ground black pepper, to taste
- ½ cup scallions, sliced crosswise

Preparation:

1. In a large, heavy-bottomed sauté pan heated over medium heat, heat 1 Tbsp of the olive oil to shimmering, then saute the shallots, corn and peppers until the shallots are soft and translucent. Stir in the thyme while cooking.
2. Transfer the shallots and corn to a bowl, then heat the remaining olive oil until shimmering. Add the shrimp to the pan and cook until the shrimp turns pink and firm, the return the shallots and corn to the pan. Stir to mix and reheat the shallots and corn. Season with the salt and pepper, to taste.
3. Stir the shrimp mixture into the grits, then transfer the mixture to a serving platter. Garnish with the scallions and serve.

Oven-Roasted Brussels Sprouts

Ingredients:

- 2 cups Brussels sprouts, trimmed and halved
- 2 Tbsp extra virgin olive oil
- 1 Tbsp paprika
- ½ Tbsp granulated garlic
- ½ tsp Kosher salt
- ½ tsp coarsely ground black pepper

Preparation:

1. Preheat the oven to 400° F.
2. In a medium-sized mixing bowl, combine the Brussles spouts with the olive oil. Toss to coat.
3. In a separate small bowl, combine the paprika, garlic, salt and pepper. Mix thoroughly.
4. Working in small batches, coat the Brussels sprouts with the spices and place on a cookie sheet.
5. Roast the Brussels sprouts for 12 to 15 minutes until fork-tender. Remove to a platter and serve.

Suggested Accompaniment:

- **Chardonnay:** Chateau St. Michelle Indian Wells (Columbia Valley, Washington)

Oven Roasted Brussels Sprouts Mixed Greens w/Pickled Mushroom
Shrimp & Grits w/Shallots, Corn and Scallions

Bog Monsters

The turkey season was almost a month old, and neither David nor I had harvested anything. Temperatures were rising, the bog in which we were hunting had dried up considerably, and we weren't hearing any toms gobbling. Even so, being in the woods was infinitely better than just about anything else we could think of, so shortly before dawn we began the short hike to our respective blinds.

The routine was the same – drop our guns and backpacks in our blinds, put out decoys, then settle in to begin calling as the morning light brightened the glade. I blew on a crow call, hoping to 'shock' any toms in the area to gobble back. Nothing.

David had decided on a similar strategy, hooting loudly from his blind a hundred yards to my right. Still nothing, so we both began yelping and clucking, hoping to entice a tom to come looking for the feeding hens who were making all the noise.

An hour had passed, and the morning light had illuminated the swamp bottom enough to reveal a little fog hugging the ground. It was a peaceful scene, but the fog would definitely make it more difficult to see any approaching birds. After a cup of coffee and a granola bar, I resumed yelping softly.

David had apparently either dozed off or left his blind to stretch his legs, because I hadn't heard any calls from his direction for over a half hour. "Oh well," I thought, "more for me!"

I waited about ten minutes after a round of yelping and clucking, then struck my box call again. Was that movement across the bog? I couldn't tell because of the light fog, so I began a series of very light clucks and feeding calls.

Sure enough, a big tom was making his way toward the decoys and my blind, stopping to raise his impressive fan every few yards! As he came closer, I was fixated on his bright blue head and red wattle. By this time, I had slowed the calling to one or two light clucks every three or four minutes.

Suddenly, he stopped and craned his head to get a better look at the decoys. He didn't speak, but I could tell that he was beginning to doubt his chances for love from these hens! Even so, he took a tentative step or two closer, then strutted and gobbled, hoping the hens would come running to him.

When the decoy hens didn't move, he lowered his fan and started to turn slowly away. I had ranged the distances to several key trees and shrubs, and knew that he was about forty-five yards out – on the very edge of my gun's limit. I squeezed the trigger and was happily surprised that he collapsed in his tracks!

Knowing that turkeys have a bad habit of not knowing when they are supposed to be dead and running off into the underbrush, I quickly exited my blind and picked my way across the semi-dry swamp, reaching the big bird as he flapped his last.

By this time, it was getting quite warm, and I was thinking that it was probably time to pack it up and head home. So, after dropping the bird and gun at my blind, I turned to retrieve the decoys.

If you've ever had the feeling of a 'sixth sense,' you'll appreciate what happened next: about fifteen yards or so from the blind, something I couldn't explain caused me to stop in my tracks. I carefully scanned the ground around me, and – sure enough! – a large cane-break rattlesnake lay to my left coiled in a slight depression in the pine needles! It was about eight feet from me, so I wasn't in danger of being struck at this point, but I wasn't about to find out how far he could strike!

Looking around, I spotted a dead pine branch a few feet to my right. I picked it up and turned toward the snake – which was apparently sleeping. I lifted the branch over my head and swung it down toward the snake's head. Rather than hitting the snake, however, the branch broke off in my hands and clattered to the forest floor! I saw the snake begin to stir and quickly looked for another branch.

The second branch I found was much sturdier, and the snake hadn't yet figured out what had awakened it. I raised this branch over my head and swung it down less violently to avoid having it break again.

The end of the branch struck the snake on the top of the head, causing it to recoil into a writhing mass. I knew it was dead, but I backed away to wait for the death throes to subside. Snakes, however, have a unique feature in that their muscles can spasm for hours after they are killed, even enabling them to bite! So, I waited until the writhing had lessened enough to pin the head under a forked stick I found nearby.

Photo by Mark Bailey – Courtesy of Alabama Fish & Game

Still trembling from the adrenaline, I carefully scanned the rest of the area in case another snake was around, then retrieved my decoys.

About twenty minutes later, with the decoys stowed in the blind and my gear in my backpack, I returned to the snake. It was still twitching, but was nearly done. Using my shooting sticks, I carefully looped a length of cord around its neck and pulled it tight, then lifted the snake into the mesh decoy bag. Still aware that a spasm could cause a fang to scratch me, I tied the decoy bag to the end of the shooting sticks like a hobo pack to carry the snake out of the woods.

When I reached the car, David was already there, sipping on a cold soda and chewing on his favored cheese and crackers.

"I heard you shoot, and I see the bird you shot" he said, "but it took you a long time after that to get here."

"Well," I replied, "there's a good reason for that! There are monsters in that bog!"

Red Onion Tart

Ingredients:

- 4 medium or 6 large Red Onions, halved crosswise, then halved vertically
- 2 Tbsp butter
- 2 Tbsp olive oil
- 2 tsp Kosher salt
- 4 tsp sugar
- 2 tsp fresh or 1 tsp dried thyme, divided
- 1 sheet thawed puff pastry

Preparation:

1. Preheat oven to 400 F.
2. In a 9" cast iron or oven-proof stainless steel pan, heat the oil and butter to sizzling over medium high heat.
3. Arrange the onion halves in the pan in a pinwheel shape. Fill the center with additional halves, or cut additional halves into quarters to fill the center. Sprinkle the salt, then the sugar evenly over the onions, then finish with half of the thyme.
4. Saute the onions for about 7 minutes, then remove the pan from the burner.
5. Lay the puff pastry sheet over the top of the pan, and trim the corners, before putting the pan into the oven.
6. Bake for about 30 minutes, or until the pastry is golden brown, then remove from the oven.
7. Place a cutting board large enough to cover the pan over the pan, then invert it onto a solid surface. Tap the bottom of the pan firmly until the tart comes loose.
8. Sprinkle the tart with the remaining thyme, then slide it onto a serving plate or platter. Serve warm.

Braised Fennel, Carrots and Apples

Ingredients:

- 1 Tbsp olive oil
- 2 cups fennel bulb, washed and cut cross-wise into ¼ inch slices
- 2 cups carrots, washed, peeled and cut into thin 2 inch strips
- 1 cup red onion, washed, peeled and coarsely chopped
- 2 cups Granny Smith apples, washed, cored and thinly sliced
- ½ cup apple cider
- ¼ cup apple cider vinegar
- ¼ cup honey
- 2 Tbsp brown mustard
- 2 Tbsp fresh basil, coarsely chopped
- Kosher salt and coarsely ground black pepper, to taste

Preparation:

1. Heat the olive oil in a medium sauté pan over medium heat and cook the fennel, carrots and onion, stirring often, until they begin to caramelize.
2. Add the apple slices, juice, vinegar, honey and mustard and stir gently to integrate. Cover and cook for 10 minutes, then uncover and cook until the liquid is absorbed and the vegetables are glazed.
3. Transfer to a serving bowl, sprinkle on the basil, salt and pepper and toss gently, then serve.

Wild Turkey Breast Terrine

Ingredients:

- 6 slices bacon
- 1 Wild Turkey breast fillet, cut into pieces
- ½ lb lean minced pork
- 1.4 cup green onions, finely chopped
- 2 garlic cloves, crushed
- ¼ cup shelled pistachio nuts
- 1 small egg, beaten
- 1 tsp poultry seasoning
- 1 tsp fennel seeds, toasted
- salt and pepper
- 2 bay leaves
- 3 thyme sprigs

Preparation:

1. Preheat oven to 350° F. Stretch the bacon slices with the back of a knife and line a small loaf tin, overlapping them slightly and leaving the edges overhanging on one side by 2 to 3 inches. Put half of the turkey into a food processor or blender and blend until finely chopped. Remove the meat to a bowl and stir in the remaining diced turkey, pork, onion, garlic, nuts, eggs, poultry seasoning, fennel seeds, and plenty of salt and pepper. Spoon the mixture into the tin, lay the bay leaves and thyme sprigs on top, then fold over the overhanging strips of bacon.

2. Cover tightly with foil. Put the loaf tin into a larger pan filled with in enough boiling water to come halfway up the side of the tin. Cook for 1½ hours. Remove the terrine from the water bath to cool, then refrigerate overnight.

3. Remove the foil, bay leaves and thyme sprigs, then place the tin in a hot water bath until the bacon begins to soften. Using a knife blade, separate the bacon from the tin, cover and flip the terrine over onto a solid surface covered with wax paper, and tap the tin until the terrine slides out onto the solid surface. Slice cross-wise and serve.

Suggested Accompaniment:

- **Savignon Blanc:** Chateau St. Michelle (Columbia Valley, Washington)
- **Chardonnay:** Toasted Head (California)

Red Onion Tart

Wild Turkey Breast Terrine

Closing Thoughts

I sincerely hope that you have enjoyed reading the adventures and trying the recipes in this book as much as I enjoyed writing and sharing them with you. Access to wild game recipes and menus are extremely limited, at best. Even with the exponential growth of the number of people interested in wild game cooking, really good resources are still relatively hard to find, so I, like a few others – Elaine Clarke and Sil Bruning, Rebecca Grey, and Scott Leysath, to name a few – appreciate the opportunity to share some of the things we've learned with those of you who appreciate the outdoors and its bounties. In doing so, I wanted the approach I chose to make you smile, bring back memories of your own, or inspire you to seek out an adventure you and your loved ones can enjoy together.

Separately, I also hope that the recipes and menus contained in these pages are interesting, delicious, nutritious, and fun to make and eat. Having evolved from a guy who used to think that over-easy eggs were a major feat to someone who loves to play in the kitchen and create 'exotic' dishes, I've tried to offer a few new ideas and ways to cook your game that will help you enjoy the preparation and presentation to your family and guests as much as you'll enjoy eating.

Finally, I hope that you'll let me know what you think of this book – the stories and photos, as well as the recipes and menus. The vast majority of what I know about preparing wild game happened because of help from others, and from old fashioned trial and error, so if I can help you avoid a few of the missteps I've already experienced – and help you avoid any wastage of your wild game – that's a good thing. And if I can learn new things from you, I'm all ears!

So, get out and live an outdoor life, then continue your adventures in the kitchen and at the dinner table!

Stan Yockey – Outdoorsman & Chef

An avid outdoorsman, Stan has hunted and fished for nearly 50 years, and is a "Life" member of the North American Hunting Club. He has harvested 6 species of big game, 5 species of small game, 15 species of upland birds, 13 species of waterfowl, over 40 species of saltwater fish, and over 25 species of fresh water fish, plus a variety of shellfish and mollusks, and has prepared an array of appetizers, salads, entrees, and side dishes showcasing his harvests – most using recipes of his own creation. Stan's outdoor pursuits have included forays with his parents, friends and family, in the Pacific Northwest in his early years, and in the Southeast over the past decade.

While growing up in Seattle, Stan worked in several respected restaurants, including The Golden Lion and The Edgewater Inn, while earning a bachelor's degree in Hotel & Restaurant Management from Washington State University. After graduating, he shifted his business focus, spending twenty years in contract management with The Boeing Company in Seattle, Washington, followed by ten years with Gulfstream Aerospace Corporation in Savannah, Georgia.

Susan, Stan's wife of over 36 years, consistently supported his outdoor and culinary endeavors, helping and encouraging him to explore new territories – both outdoors and in the kitchen. Embracing this support, Stan penned his first cookbook, "A Life Outdoors (and In the Kitchen!)" to capture many of his adventures and provides recipes and menu recommendations based on the game featured in each story. One of these adventures, "Walleye Encounters," is featured in the Summer 2012 issue of "Cooking Wild" magazine; several adventures and menus were later featured in "Richmond Hill Reflections" – a local magazine in Richmond Hill, Georgia.

Stan currently divides his time between work as a business management consultant and his continuing pursuit of outdoor and culinary adventures from his home in Hoschton, Georgia.